Praise
Don't You R...

D1193738

George Ella Lyon, in *Don't You Remember?*, goes more deeply into the mystery of the creative process than anyone I've read. She celebrates this mystery in a compelling narrative, an irresistible story filled with suspense and wonder. The writing is just lovely.

— BOBBIE ANN MASON
author of *In Country, Nancy Culpepper*
and *Clear Springs: A Memoir*

"Lyon's story is haunting, thought-provoking, brave, amazing, and maybe even the best book yet from this beloved author. No matter what you believe about past-life experiences, there's no denying that this is a book of rare beauty and excellent writing."

— SILAS HOUSE
author of *Clay's Quilt, The Coal Tattoo*
and *A Parchment of Leaves*

As enthralling as any mystery story – for it is a mystery story of the highest order – *Don't You Remember?* enlists the reader in a search for the source of many puzzling "memories" and unexplained coincidences in George Ella Lyon's life. This search will take her up and down one continent and across to another, opening up possibilities of story and mystery which speak to us all.

— LEE SMITH
author of *The Last Girls, On Agate Hill*
and *Fair and Tender Ladies*

Though I've never had a glimmer of a past-life experience myself, I found this account of George Ella Lyon's encounter riveting, as suspenseful as a good mystery. But the stakes are much higher. Only a person deeply at home in her own spirit could have had this experience, much less written about it with such trustworthy discernment, such willingness to be led into and through what was happening to her, such luminous clarity. It is also, as it happens, a penetrating, serious meditation on the kind of possession – by impulse, intuition, memory – through which fiction of the best kind arises.

— MARY ANN TAYLOR-HALL
author of *How She Knows What She Knows About Yo-Yos*
and *Come and Go, Molly Snow*

Don't You Remember?

A Memoir

George Ella Lyon

Don't You Remember?
A Memoir

by George Ella Lyon

ISBN   0-9778745-6-7

Cover photo by Algieri Images: www.algieri-images.co.uk
Cover design by Kurt Gohde: www.kurtgohde.com
Layout design by EK LARKEN

Published in Louisville, Kentucky USA, by

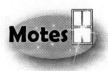

an imprint of

EvaMedia
PO Box 6034
Louisville KY   40206-0034

WWW.MOTESBOOKS.COM

Acknowledgments

Earlier versions of excepts from this book appeared in *The American Voice* and *Ace Magazine.*

My research and writing were made possible, in part, by a grant from The Kentucky Foundation for Women and an Al Smith Fellowship from the Kentucky Arts Council. I am deeply grateful for this support.

Even deeper thanks goes to my husband Steve, who believed in this project from the beginning; to Ann Olson, who accompanied me at the outset of the journey; to the woman I consulted about past lives; to Kitty Pierce; to my writers group and Pat Hudson, who read and commented on multiple incarnations of this manuscript; to friends and family who encouraged me; to Kurt Gohde and Deborah Kessler for their work on the design; and to Kate, who took it on and saw it through.

In the interest of privacy, I have changed some names but not those which were the object of my search.

For my sons,
Benn and Joey

Calling

In the belly of the ship
in the bell of the sea
come to me
Take the rocking road

Life within life
kicks at my backbone
Life beyond life
beats in your heart

I shall lose this baby
so quick within me
I shall go empty
into new life
but by the pulse
racing through my wrist
by her foot
that will never feel a floor
You are mine too

The sea is rough
and I am cold tonight
Sing to me, little music

1

I was forty-six when I began this journey, a poet, a wife and mother, a spiritual seeker. I make my living as a children's writer and free-lance teacher. Originally from the Appalachian mountains, I live in the south or midwest, depending on what you call Kentucky. I have two sons, three cats, ninety journals, and a PhD. Mostly I hide the PhD, though. It puts people off.

I have a double name and, more than that, a double-gendered name: George Ella. Sometimes I think my mother sealed my fate when she named me for her brother and sister, names which go far back in the family but had always been dealt out along gender lines before. I get to be both. To explain to people that yes, I am the person they are expecting. No man is going to show up. To be a joke on the maternity ward. Thank you very much.

Really, I do thank her. She made me word conscious even about my name. She gave me paradox in the crib.

I also arrived with an eye condition which produced double vision, a doubleness that echoed my name. While I knew only half of what I saw was real, it was still hard to determine which half.

When I started school, I found out my name was odd, but I didn't learn about my vision. Like all children, I thought everyone saw the world the way I did: two of everything, with the ghost image slightly higher and tilted to the right. Somehow other people just managed better – not running into things, not reading the lesson out loud twice. I didn't discover the truth till I was in the fifth grade. But that's a different story.

Double vision is like my name in another way: perhaps it points to a deeper divergence of seeing – past and present, spirit and matter, living and dead. Perhaps I had early lessons in the truth that there's more to our lives, to us, than meets the eye.

Maybe I'm just now accepting this. Maybe I'm telling myself as I tell you.

2

It was my father's death which sent me in search of this story. On December 15, 1986, Daddy died, a month to the day after my second son was born. In the birthing room, I had pushed open the bone gate and let a soul into the world. Minutes later, this new being latched onto my breast. He had made it through and was anchored.

Thirty days later in intensive care, as Daddy's body let go its hold on life, another gate opened, invisible. His lungs shut; his heart stilled: no earthly tie could keep him. Though we held his solid hands, his soul slipped free.

But halfway between these two days came a moment at St. Mary's, when the Sisters sneaked the baby past hospital rules so that the two could meet. Both were alert, Daddy still in his own room, conscious though he couldn't speak. He'd been a big man – six feet tall and ample – but now, at 5'2" and twelve days postpartum, I outweighed him.

Light shone from him, though. A radiance I'd never seen before. I walked to the bed and held Joey up. What happened then I cannot reach with words: how their eyes met equally ancient and new, Joey's and Daddy's, knowing each other, before and after, holding each other in their passing. Myself, sunk in time like a tree, as all I could bear of Beyond opened.

CR

Twenty years have passed since that moment, but the door to Beyond has never entirely closed. Or maybe it never is closed. Maybe what I witnessed between Joey and Daddy tuned me to its opening so that now and then I am able to see through.

For a long time I thought of these glimpses as isolated incidents. You're a writer, I told myself. They come with the territory. For example, I dreamed of an acquaintance of Daddy's, someone I'd never met and hadn't thought about in years. The next morning I wrote a poem from the dream, and that night learned that he had been murdered. This scared me so much I threw the poem away. Another morning I wrote about a character being shown an old photograph of some-one who looks uncannily like her. When the mail arrived later that day, it brought a large envelope with a note from a friend which said, "I found this old picture of my great aunt. Doesn't she look like you?" "Wait a minute!" I thought. "I just wrote that!"

While I didn't dismiss these experiences, I didn't re-ally look at them either. But then came one that I couldn't ignore.

I wrote a monologue for a play in my great-great grand-mother, Ester Bruton's voice. I did this by recalling the few things I knew about her and then by listening, in my imagination and my heart, for her voice and writing it down. Ester tells of traveling by horseback, six months pregnant with my great grandmother, to bring her dying husband home from the Civil War. In the monologue, she speaks of two other children, a girl and a younger boy, left with neighbors as she set off on her journey. I thought I had made them up, but a month later, when a copy of her pension application arrived from the National Archives, I found those two children listed! Searching the document for other connections, I saw it was dated December 15th, the day of my father's death.

Unnerving as that was, I might have let it go, but a year later, a Christmas card addressed to Ms. Ester arrived at our house. It was from someone in New York City I'd never heard of. How could this be? Our house was only fifty years old and we had a list of the previous owners. There was no Ester.

I wrote to the senders, whose name was Peralta, explaining that no Ester lived at our house but that it was a family name. I asked how they got our address.

They didn't respond, so after six weeks I called them. I knew it would seem strange but it *was* strange.

Mrs. Peralta, who had written the card, wasn't home, but her husband told me, in a rich accent I couldn't place, that yes, he remembered my note. Ester was their young friend. After her marriage, she had moved to Lexington and given them my address. Because they couldn't remember her new last name, his wife had written only Ester. But they'd wanted to find out how she was faring in her new life, especially because when she left New York she was pregnant.

Pregnant?

While I had been writing about my Ester's pregnant journey, the Peraltas believed a pregnant Ester was traveling to live in my house.

"Don't worry," I wanted to say to Mr. Peralta. "Ester's fine. The baby's fine. In fact, she's going to be my great grandmother."

But I just thanked him and hung up.

Then I walked to my dining room and looked out at the wintry yard. There was no earthly explanation for what had just happened. I had asked the only people who could provide one. The door to Beyond stood ajar and again the light had flashed into my eyes. That was all. All.

Except that when I slipped the card back in its envelope I caught sight of the postmark: December 15th.

If you put such synchronicity into fiction, readers would call it forced, unbelievable. But it was happening. I wasn't making it up.

It was making me up.

So nine years after my father died I said Enough. If strangeness was going to keep coming after me, I would turn around and face it. More than that, I would go toward it. I would approach the strangest thing that ever happened to me. I would return to the town where as a small child I had seemed to remember another life.

3

I was scared to go back to Bath, New York, that town my family passed through on vacation when I was five. Was I saying to the spirit world, "Here I am. Come and get me?" Was I volunteering to go off the deep end? Would people think I was crazy? Was I crazy?

I knew better than to go alone. If I was going to encounter something from another life I needed someone from this life to keep me centered. My husband couldn't do it. He had to stay home to work and take care of the kids.

So I asked my friend Ann. She's steady, practical. Also imaginative, open. A photographer and writer. When I told her how I felt compelled to return to Bath, she said, "Isn't that *interesting*?" and meant it. Non-judgmental. Tall and confident. Easy to find if you get lost. She'd be the anchor person as I scaled this unknown cliff. She'd see that I didn't fall out of time.

Ann was headed to parents' weekend at her daughter's school and I had a job in Pennsylvania. When the conference where I spoke was over, she picked me up and we drove out of

York in a sudden storm that ended in a double rainbow.

"Look!" I exclaimed, as Ann navigated streams of rain and traffic. "That's only the second time I've seen one of those."

"Wow!" she said, bending over the steering wheel to see the soft colored arcs blessing the horizon.

Double. Double rainbow. "It's a good sign," I said, partly joking. I didn't want to start latching onto signs. You can read rice stuck to the bottom of the pot if you want to.

Really and truly, that was my dilemma: I didn't want to go too far. I still don't. I don't want you to think I'm crazy. I don't want to be crazy. If crazy is somewhere you go, I want to head in the opposite direction. I don't want to look ridiculous either.

Oh boy. If I'm holding fast to sanity with one hand and grasping all I have of dignity with the other, how am I going to receive? And how can I steady myself going forward?

Ann drove north under clearing skies through Wilkes-Barre, Binghamton, and into the Corning area. I was getting shaky with excitement as we turned onto Highway 17.

"This is where it started," I said. "Near Painted Post."

"Tell it again."

"Not now. Right now I just want to watch and see what I feel."

We grew quiet. The blue van moved on the gray road between tawny fields, under crimson and gold trees and azure sky.

"We're in a postcard," I said. But that was the only thing odd about the road. I didn't feel any shivers or glimpse anything familiar as we drove. I felt self-conscious since I was the instrument I kept checking, but what else could I do?

Finally we came to Bath itself, which was another kind of postcard: the perfect roomy open neat small town, a park with a fountain in the center of the square; old, well-kept buildings – city hall, hotel, newspaper office and churches surrounding it.

"Is that the fountain?" Ann asked, as we pulled into one of the diagonal parking slots nearby.

"I guess so," I said, climbing out.

Standing by the white-washed blue-lined pool, which is not much bigger than those you inflate for kids in the back-yard, I put my hand in the water.

"This is it," I said. "We all sat here."

"Tell the story," Ann insisted. And as we walked the paths of the little park, I did.

❧

If I was five, my brother Robert was almost twelve, my mother thirty-four, my father thirty-six. We were en route from our home in the Kentucky mountains to Niagara Falls, where my parents had spent their honeymoon.

It was 1954. If you turned on the radio you might hear Rosemary Clooney singing "Hey There." But I could sing it when the radio was off. I knew all the words. Just as Robert knew the stats for the Yankees, I knew songs. So as we drove that morning up Highway 17, I was singing. I was singing as we passed Painted Post, but all of a sudden I stopped.

"Daddy," I said. "Blow the horn under the underpass!" This was one of our traditions.

"I would, Sugar," he said, "but there isn't any underpass here."

"There will be," I told him. Then we went around a curve and there it was.

Daddy laid on the horn. I loved the echo.

A mile or so later Robert spotted a big building in the distance. "What's that?" he asked.

"Can't tell from here," Daddy said. "Maybe we'll pass it."

"It's a razor blade factory," I said.

"What?" Mother asked, turning around in her seat.

"It's a razor blade factory," I said again.

"Where does she get such ideas?" Mother asked Daddy.

But when we got close, they saw it was a razor blade factory.

"Whoa!" Robert said. "How did you know that?" We hadn't passed a sign back there and anyway I couldn't read.

But I was on another tack now. "Can we go see the fountain?" I asked. "I want to see the fountain." I was excited, bouncing up and down in the seat.

"What fountain?" Daddy asked.

"The one in the park," I answered.

"What park?" Robert asked.

"The one with round lights on a stem," I said, holding my arms out like the branches of the lamp, palms downward, cupped to hold globes of glass.

It may have been the lamps that got them. We didn't have any like that in my hometown. Or maybe we were all in a trance by now. Or maybe Daddy was more curious than afraid.

"Do you know how to get to this park?" he asked.

"Turn up there," I told him.

And, as if I'd been giving directions in Bath, New York, all my life, I guided him through the few turns till we pulled up at the park.

"There's the lamps," Daddy said.

"And the fountain," Mother put in.

They let me run around the little park, my plump legs brown in plaid shorts, the white ruffle of my halter top flapping. I touched the lamp posts, the trees, the gazebo. I did somersaults in the grass. Finally I came to sit by them at the fountain. Robert was measuring the depth of the water with a stick.

"Is this where you wanted to come, Sugar?" Daddy asked. He was sweating. It was July and he still wore long pants and a tee shirt under his sport shirt.

"Um-hmm," I said. It felt so good to be there.

"How did you know about this place?" Mother asked.

"I used to teach school here," I told them.

Now if we had just been driving through the town and I had said that, they might have laughed it off. But coming as it did after I'd predicted landmarks and led them to the park, it was, well, creepy.

"Where?" Daddy asked.

And I gave them directions to the school. After that little jaunt, they decided to get some lunch to steady their nerves, so we ducked into a nearby restaurant. Right after we'd ordered, Mother got up to find the restroom.

"Watch out for the steps," I said.

We'd just begun to sip from our drinks when she

21

reappeared.

"Let's go," she said firmly.

"Go?" Daddy asked.

"Let's go home," she said, coming down hard on the last word.

"Gladys, honey, sit down," Daddy coaxed. "What's wrong?"

She perched sideways on her chair. She didn't put her feet under the table.

"When I opened the door," she said, "the light was out. And there were stairs straight down. No warning sign. I would have fallen if . . . if . . . I want to get out of this place! I want to go home!"

"That's what we'll do then," Daddy said, mild as always. "We'll pack up our lunch as soon as it comes and – "

"No!" Mother said, and stood up. "We have to go now."

And we did. The way they tell it, we drove straight back to Harlan. No motel. We didn't even stop to eat. We had a cooler and a sack of groceries Mother replenished at a little market. They got take-out coffee. The engine didn't really cool off till we got home.

Ironically, I don't remember any of this. I didn't even hear the story till I was in college and I wouldn't have heard it then if I hadn't been driving with Robert and Betty, his wife, and just for nostalgia's sake, asked Robert to blow the horn as we approached a concrete tunnel under the railroad.

"Remember when you wanted Dad to blow the horn and there wasn't any underpass?" Robert asked.

"No," I said.

"And you told him there would be and around the next curve there was?"

"What?"

"You were only five," he said.

I leaned forward over the front seat of his Ford Galaxie. "Robert, what are you talking about?"

"Don't you remember?" he said.

4

"But of course, I didn't," I told Ann. "And he wouldn't tell me. I had to ask our parents the next time I was home from college."

"And?"

"Oh, they looked at each other – that parent look that remembers and calculates and decides – and then they told me."

"How long ago was that?" Ann asked.

"Twenty-five years, more or less."

"And you're just now getting here? Weren't you curious? I think I would have come right then."

"I didn't have a car!"

"I would have borrowed one," she said.

"Maybe," I told her. "But there was all this secrecy about it, like there was shame mixed up in the weirdness of it all. Nobody wanted to talk about it. I wasn't supposed to know. Even now I feel some of that."

"We better go check in at the hotel then," Ann said. "Before you back out."

I'd made reservations at the Old National Hotel, right across the street from the square, so we just got our suitcases and bookbags from the van and walked over.

When we entered the slant-floored lobby, Ann raised her eyebrows and I shook my head. It didn't look familiar. It had character though. If I didn't remember it when I got there, I would when I left.

The registration counter was dark wood, a little dusty. I gave the clerk my name, he looked up the card and asked, "What brings you to Bath?"

This caught me off guard.

"Business or pleasure?" he went on.

"Genealogical research," I said, relieved to have come up with something.

"You should stay over till Monday then," he said. "All the record offices are closed on the weekend."

I smiled. "There's the library."

"Closes in two hours," he said.

"Thanks." He took my credit card, then gave me the key. Was he being aggressive or was I just defensive?

Ann and I climbed the slightly slanted stairs in silence.

"I hadn't thought about how awkward this was going to be," I told her as we unpacked in our big dim room.

"Maybe you should just say we're visiting," she suggested.

"It's a small town. They'll want to know who."

"Right," she said, carrying shampoo and toothpaste into the tiny black and white tiled bathroom.

"And if I say I'm writing a book, they'll ask about that

25

too."

"So make something up," Ann said.

"If I say I'm researching an ancestor – which is true, sort of, isn't it? –" Ann nodded. "Then they'll want a name or at least a time period."

She nodded again.

"And I don't have any of these things . . ."

Ann folded back the white chenille spread on one of the beds and stretched out. Springs creaked. "Slightly dippy," she reported.

"My story?"

She laughed. "Just see what you see," she said. "You can always ask about the razor blade factory."

After a little rest we took a walk. I wanted to look at the school, which was closed, too, of course. I wanted to read the vibrations of the town. If anything, Bath was too perfect: a movie set of a small town, all clean and freshly painted, sparkling in the October afternoon light. We found out that they had recently celebrated their bicentennial and everything had been spruced up for that occasion. It was impressive and pleasant, but for someone looking for a connection with the past, it felt like they'd sprayed the whole place with emotional Teflon.

At dinner in The Octopus' Garden (where I checked for steps down to the restroom – they didn't have them), I asked the waitress, who looked to be about my age, if she remembered a razor blade factory. She didn't, but volunteered to call an old-timer for me. I was surprised. Business wasn't that slow either. When she got Mr. Wallace on the line, I went to the phone by the cash register and tried to hear him over

26

the din of silverware and conversation. No, he said. He was sorry but he didn't know of such a place. But he was more interested in family history than the economic side. If I had a name –

I thanked him and went back to the table.

"Maybe your folks remembered it wrong," Ann said, when I told her what happened.

"But *razor blade factory* is so specific," I said. "Why would they come up with that?"

Between bites of broiled flounder Ann said, "Did he ask why you wanted to know?"

"No."

"Neither did the waitress," she pointed out. "I don't think you have to worry."

"It's this bicentennial," I told her, just figuring it out. "They're all primed for questions."

Back in the hotel after dinner, I decided to call Robert. Maybe if he tried he could remember something else from that long-ago trip, some detail that would give me a clue about what to do next.

Betty answered the phone. I told her where I was and that I wanted to ask Robert some questions. There was no *Hello* when he came on the line. He just said, "Go home!"

"I'm not staying long," I assured him. "Just tell me what you remember."

He recounted the story of the underpass, the razor blade factory, the park, the lunch. But he thought we'd already been to Niagara Falls and came through Bath on our way home.

That's strange, I thought. Either we went or we didn't. But I didn't linger over this question. I decided to call it a night and check out churches in the morning. Maybe I'd find something there.

CR

The first service was morning prayer at St. Thomas Episcopal. No music, no wine, no connection, just words dry as bread crumbs in a chilly stone chapel.

The next was at the First Presbyterian which had brilliant windows, a Tiffany chandelier, and a robust choir taking arpeggios to Heaven. I enjoyed it, but as a spectator only.

The last stop was St. Mary's, the little Catholic Church just down Morris Street from the square. The small sanctuary was crowded. I arrived as folks were standing to go to communion. Singing, too, their hands crossed and cupped in front of them to receive the body and blood. I had to step past a man kneeling by the doorway to get in.

And when I did that, when I brushed past him, it was as if I walked off the deep end of a pool and plunged into grief. It was over my head in an instant.

I, who never cry in public, who rarely cry in front of anyone, started sobbing. People turned to look at me, a stranger falling apart in the aisle of their church. But they were not as shocked as I was. I had no earthly idea why I was crying. I just felt sorrow and loss welling up, huge and unstoppable. I tried to get hold of myself, standing without story or Kleenex in the line for communion.

At the end of Mass I asked the priest some questions, but having seen me distraught at the altar, he seemed wary. Yes, they had a school but it wasn't founded till 1961; no, there was no church historian. "Excuse me, " he said, twitching his alb. "I have to leave to say Mass at another church."

Wrung out and bewildered, I walked back up Morris Street and met Ann in the park. After a morning of photography, she had the van loaded, ready to go.

"You won't believe what happened," I told her as we drove out of town. "It was incredible."

But I couldn't describe the total strangeness of being overtaken with feeling and not having a clue as to what it was about. It was as if my emotional self had been replaced when I walked into the sanctuary, but the new one – or perhaps the old one – was not hooked up to my understanding. It just expressed itself and was gone, leaving me struggling for words in the front seat of a Toyota van.

Was this what had happened when I was five? Someone's consciousness just replaced mine for a time, telling what it remembered, expressing its desire to see the park? It wasn't sorrowful then; it was eager, determined. And I was open; I didn't second-guess myself. I let it speak.

"They weren't my tears," I kept saying to Ann as we drove east.

"So whose were they?" she asked.

"The schoolteacher's, I guess."

"And who was she?"

"I don't know. But I feel like I've got to find out."

"How?" Ann asked.

5

I wrestled with that question all fall and into the new year. Research I could do. I had my graduate-school library skills and the county-court-clerk ones I'd developed when working on the play about Ester. But you have to have something – a name, a date, a family – to look up. All I had were two very odd experiences and some witnesses.

By January, I had come up with only one research method: I could go to past-life therapy. I didn't believe in past lives, mind you. I didn't know anyone who did. And I didn't know if there was a past-life therapist in the territory. But assuming I found one, what did I have to lose?

Dignity, sanity, money, my concept of myself as someone too – what? intelligent? Christian? educated? skeptical? – too *something* to fall for such a deluded idea. I had plenty of other things to do, thank you: mothering things like driving the car pool, chaperoning Cub Scouts, volunteering at my son's school; and writer things – getting my own work done, leading workshops, appearing as a visiting author in enough schools to make a living. I had a house to keep, a yard to dig in. I sang in the church choir. I didn't need this, for heaven's sake. My plate was full.

But the memory of that morning in St. Mary's would not let me rest. Something real had met me there, an expression of the very thing I had gone back for. I couldn't just forget it. I had to keep searching.

Now they don't list past-life therapists in the Yellow Pages, not in Lexington, Kentucky, anyway, so I called the local Unitarian minister and asked if she knew of one. Not only did she give me a name, she recommended this woman, who was also a lawyer in town. I wrote down the information, but I was still torn. It took me two more months to make the call.

CR

Laura's office was in a stone-and-brick turn of the century (that would be the 20th) house in the elegant part of downtown. Big trees, high windows, arched porches. The wide hall and waiting room, which served several offices, were painted a light, noncommittal green and furnished with similar couches and chairs, the chief aim of their design being not to clash with anything. (I could be describing myself here.)

When my appointment time came, Laura opened the pocket doors to her office and revealed another world: black and red, midnight blue, parrot yellow, iridescent green: paintings, chairs, carvings, weavings, sculpture – everything alive with color and imagery. I took a deep breath and stepped over the threshold.

For an hour we sat and talked. I told my story and Laura explained that five was the most common age for past-

31

life memories to surface because the child is old enough to be articulate, yet young enough not to be self-conscious. She also said that the car ride itself could have contributed.

"You know how babies often fall asleep in the car?" she said.

"Sure. I drove my first one many a mile for that very reason."

"Well, that's because the steady motion can put you in a light trance."

Then she told me that if I chose to come back, she would induce a similar state through relaxation and guided imagery exercises. "You won't lose touch with who and where you are," Laura assured me, "but you'll be in another time, too. Once that happens, all I do is ask questions. And I tape the session so you can hear it again when you go home."

I looked at this tall slender woman, who with her blue-black hair, intense eyes, turquoise dress and purple jacket, was as vivid as the nest she'd made. She seemed stable, professional, very much in this world. She was a lawyer, recommended by a minister. I decided to trust her. To trust myself. And this process. After all, I didn't understand how writing worked either. I made a living from uncertainty. And if it didn't feel right after the first session, I could always back out.

Still, it wasn't easy. Always the brownest bird of the hedge, I couldn't believe I was signing on for trance travel in a South American dreamscape. Not only did it cost $75 for an hour and a half, Laura made it clear that I might not arrive in Bath right away. "You've had many lives," she said. "You have many stories to tell."

"Okay," I said, shaking like one of those hedge leaves. If I knew another path, I'd take it. But since I didn't, I told her to put me down for the next Thursday at 2:00. A date, a time, a place. So be it.

6

I vacillated through the week before that second appointment. How did I turn into a person who would go to past-life therapy? Wasn't I grounded in the real world? Didn't I teach an Education for Ministry class at church? What would my students think? My friends? My children?

It's clear now that part of me wanted everything to stay the same while another part was ready, even yearning, to step out into the unknown. Throughout the search, these two forces have been pulling me – one drawing me on, another holding me back. They are with me as I write this today. And while I long to throw myself wholeheartedly forward, I see that this back-and-forth way of going is necessary. It weaves my old consciousness to the new; it prevents me from changing so fast that I desert myself. A wise woman told me, "Reach out only as far as the outreach is solid." So I think my double-mindedness may be a strength rather than a weakness, a way of making sure of good ground underfoot.

Solid ground is very important when, after relaxing on a futon for about ten minutes, after visualizing yourself walking down a country road and across a bridge, you find yourself truly transported. "Look down at your feet," Laura says. "What are you wearing?"

And in your mind's eye – you're wearing a blindfold – you look down and see:

a little girl's feet in green stockings and brown shoes

or

an old man's gnarled and dusty bare black feet

or

a woman's slim feet in gray high-button shoes.

It doesn't matter how hokey you thought this whole process was when you lay down. Once you cross the bridge you are changed. When Laura asks what your clothing is like, you know because you can see it. You know what kind of hair you have and what you're carrying.

"Go to the place where you'll sleep tonight," Laura says, "and when you get there, tell me what you see."

You know that, too, whether it's the little bed tucked under the window in the loft of the cottage or the clear spot as far from the fire as you can throw your spear. Once you've found and described this place – your home at that point of entry into this life – Laura continues, "Now go forward or backward in time to a significant moment and, when you get there, tell me what happens."

There is no hesitation. With the same ease you would show in describing central events in your current life, you know these moments, whether you're a Native American girl caught in a grass fire, an Asian boy tasting a copper bowl, or a New York schoolteacher unmarried and trapped in 1873.

Laura was right. It took many sessions before I arrived in the story I was looking for. "Well, of course," you may think. "That's how people in this business make more money." But that's because you're thinking about this in a rational way, and the experience isn't rational. Is this a story relived from the collective unconsious? my psyche's creation of a mirror-life? an actual visit to a previous existence? I do not know. My only claim is that the stories I experienced through this process felt true as I was telling them, felt they were mine in a different way from stories I write, and that living with the stories afterward changed my life.

CR

The Bath schoolteacher I was seeking didn't always tell the truth, as it turns out. She didn't lie: she just left out crucial facts, not for my benefit but because the second half of her life had been built on secrets, and tending secrets gets into your blood. Even beyond blood, into your essence.

She told her story out of order, from different points in her life, over six sessions. Her mother's name was Lucy, her father's work was with machines. When he became ill, she left school to work in his office and to help take care of him. After his death she took teacher training and stayed on in the family home as companion and support of her mother, her brother

36

having married and moved away.

In great agitation she tells of a turning point in her life. This is an excerpt from the transcript:

It's raining. Very hard. (long pause) The last leaves are being torn off the trees.

Where are you?

I'm walking outside. I don't know why I feel such sadness, but something is very heavy. I can see clouds rolling in the sky. It's cold. It feels like things are being torn apart. Doors are being shut. Like I'm walking away from something.

What happens next?

(She hesitates. This is the longest silence on the tape.) There's a package, there's something tied up with string. It's on the porch when I get, when I get home.

Is this the same house that you grew up in?

Umhmm.

What happens next?

I take it in. The cat comes in too. There's a chill in the house. My mother's lying down. My father has died.

Has he died recently or some time ago?

Some time ago. And my mother has what she calls the vapors and has these spells and lies down. I go back to the kitchen. Take a dipper of water. I'm wet to the skin, yet I'm thirsty. I take a knife and cut the string on the package. I unwrap it on the drainboard as if it were a piece of meat.

And what's inside that package?

(long pause) It's a little, it's a little book. It's a little – it's in a case like a diploma or a passport.

Do you know what this thing is? Is it something you've sent for or asked for?

I think it is. I think (long pause), I think I have to leave.

You have to leave where?

I have to leave home now.

Okay. In looking at this thing that looks like a diploma or a passport, can you see your name on it anywhere?

I see a seal, embossed.

Look to see if you can see your name written or typed there.

I think it says Joan. Or Jane.

Does it have a last name on it?

(pause) There's a word, Grace. But that might be Grace Joan. Or Jane Grace. I don't know.

Okay. Allow yourself to become aware of why it is that you're going to be leaving and as those memories begin to occur, just go ahead and report whatever you think. Or feel.

I have to go because I can't breathe. I have to go because I stayed, I stayed to take care of my father and I thought when he was gone, then my life would begin, but I see now that I'll be taking care of my mother and it won't be a time to begin. It will be too late to begin if I don't go now. But this is wrong. For me to do this.

I sent a letter to my brother and told him, told him to come now and do his part, but he's married and there are children. I tried to talk to my mother about it. I couldn't find the words. Everything I would say was so raw. And it had no shell of words like *duty* around it that she could bear to hear from me. To say *I, I want this* would crack that shell. But I have to get out. I have to break the shell. Because this is not, this is not my life.

Where will you go?

I'm going across the ocean. I've saved my money and

I'm going on a ship.

What will you do when you get there?

Probably I'll teach school. It's all I know to do. But I'll be free of all these, these stories, these roots that hold me too close. I have a little money to live on. I've sold a brooch I had. I sold a silver hairbrush and mirror. Mother hasn't missed these things. She doesn't see well and she doesn't take care of things now so she doesn't dust and see what might be moved or gone.

Because of her failing eyesight she likes to be read to. I hope someone will read to her. I can't take her with me. There's this house and I don't know what will become of it. But there's money in it for her. If the house were sold there would be money for my brother to help take care of her.

What happens next?

I make dinner. Apples and pork. And green beans. I have it all ready and I wake Mother up. And we eat in the dining room. but I have too many words stuck in my throat to eat. And she sees this. She says, "You're just rearranging your food." And so I say, "I don't feel well."

What happens next?

(pause) She says if I want to go and lie down she'll do the washing up. But I couldn't lie down. I don't want her to do that. I tell her that my brother's going to visit. And that he might come while I'm out, for her not to be upset if he comes while I'm at school tomorrow. I don't want her to be frightened. She'll be up early in the morning before I go, but I don't want to wait till then to tell her. Because I know by then that I might, my voice might give something else away, so I tell her this tonight. I say he's coming on business, but I think, what if I go and he doesn't come?

Have you told your mother you're actually going or are you just leaving?

No. She'll think I've gone to school. I told the school. I signed the paper. But I only did that this afternoon and slipped it under the office door, so no one will talk to her before tomorrow.

Okay. Go ahead and allow yourself to move forward or backward again in this lifetime to another significant event and when you're there, simply begin to talk about whatever you experience.

(pause) I'm on the coast. I'm walking along among the rocks. Sea spray. It's a beautiful gray day. It's full of the sound of the water and the birds crying. And the steep sand, rocks and little flowers. Little plants that are wonderful colors. You think first it's all just green and then you look and it's a hundred colors.

Do you know where this ocean is, where you are?

41

It's the ocean or it's the Irish Sea. This is Wales.

CR

Lying there on the black futon, under the red and turquoise afghan, I wept at leaving, wept as I had in the church in Bath. But now I had a name and a story for my tears.

I left the office by the back door and as I was walking down the concrete steps of the old house, a little snake whipped past where I was about to set my foot. My heart jumped and I caught my breath. Was this a warning – the snake in the garden, purveyor of forbidden knowledge? I had a ways to travel before I could think of the snake as it's seen in other traditions: mysterious skin-shedder, symbol of everlasting life.

7

One of the most extraordinary parts of past-life work is going through the death of the person you are remembering. It doesn't always happen, but when it does, it's unforgettable. After all, this is not an experience you expect to survive, at least not in any way you can talk about in this life. But you do survive it, not only as yourself now but as the spirit of the person you are being. And suddenly you know, know in the bones you no longer have, that the thing we most want to be true *is* true: that the soul survives! There it is, luminous and sentient and sometimes even funny, on the other side.

Yes, I know what you're thinking. Since that longing is so fundamental, of course we would let it be fulfilled in our imagined lives. I can't argue with you there. I don't want to argue. I can only tell you what I experienced.

After going through six sessions in which I explored Jane's life, I came to her death. As her spirit left her body, Laura asked me to stay with it, to move into the state between lifetimes. Eastern traditions call this Bardo, where the individual consciousness goes back to what's called the Oversoul.

This is the larger part of us which knows all our lifetimes, and it's when we are gathered in this place that we make our commitments and chose our learning for the next round of existence. The Oversoul remembers what we mostly forget at birth: who we were, what we've chosen, why we've come.

I felt free and new, released from Jane's body which had grown so heavy and still. Giddy and more like a sustained note than anything else, I entered a room that wasn't a room, where the table was the sky. Then, as if on an intake of breath, I was this larger thing, completely settled, completely free. And Laura asked, "Can you tell us anything about Jane to help us understand this lifetime?"

"There was a baby," I said.

Of course! Why hadn't I figured that out? What else could push her to make so daring, so extreme a move? She had said she left to save her life, but now I knew this wasn't a metaphor. Nor was it her life only. What choices did a woman in such a predicament in her place and time have? She could marry the father, if he were willing and available, which was highly unlikely. She might find — and probably die of — a kitchen-table abortion. Or she could disappear into another life.

CR

I couldn't disappear from mine, so I sought out a genealogist in that area of New York to comb through local archives looking for Jane Grace. The first person I hired couldn't deal with the vagueness of my search — I had a name and a place but no date — so she took her $50 and quit.

Meanwhile, my own research discovered that there had been enough immigration from Wales to western New York to result in at least two books on the subject. I ordered them.

At that point it was July, 1996, nine months after my return to Bath. I had a job scheduled in August speaking to teachers in the Catskills. Steve and Joey, who was nine, were going with me. While I taught, they'd go to the Baseball Hall of Fame at Cooperstown, and then we'd head south and east to our annual family gathering on the Outer Banks.

We didn't plan to go through Bath. I wanted to, but the trip was already crowded and I felt that it wouldn't be fair to make the guys wait around for several days while I holed up in records offices. A job was one thing, but this – what was this?

However, because of road construction, AAA routed us right through Erie, Pennsylvania, and into western New York, so that we were practically driving past the Bath courthouse. Steve and I agreed I should give it a morning.

I was nervous. I'd been nervous the fall before when I came with Ann, but this was different. Having my family with me, I was in my mothering, wifely mode, and so not fully available to myself. Because of this, I was worried that I wouldn't be open to any connections I might feel, that I'd be too hurried and distracted to do any research and, conversely, that if I *did* feel or find anything, I might react emotionally in a way which would scare Joey and which I wouldn't be able to explain to him. With work and practice, you can worry about opposite possibilities at the same time.

Through the AAA guide, I discovered an airplane museum near Bath for Steve and Joey to visit while I went to the

45

County Court Clerk's office and, time permitting, to St. Mary's. They'd pick me up at the park at noon, we'd drive through lunch and head on to Oneonta where the conference began with dinner that night.

From the outside, the Bath records office looks like a little church, and inside there was that sacred hush of old libraries, where the loudest thing you hear is the wheel rolling as a wooden file drawer is pulled out or the thump of a hefty volume laid on an oak table.

Marian Kimmer, a small woman in her seventies, presided over this shrine. Curly gray hair framed her pointed face, and she had ice-blue eyes behind sparkling glasses. When I asked for the 1850 census, she directed me to atlas-sized volumes stacked on their sides on a shelf along the far wall. The one I wanted was the color of old grass clippings and it creaked slightly as I opened it. In beautiful, many-ten-drilled script, the title page read:

1850 Census
United States of America
Steuben County
New York

You can't turn these big brittle pages in a hurry, so the speed I couldn't express with my hands went to my heart. By the time I found the *G's*, I was a little lightheaded. I ran my finger down the litany of names inscribed before the Civil War, when Walt Whitman was writing *Leaves of Grass*.

What if there weren't any Graces? Of course there wouldn't be, I told myself. This whole effort was deluded, searching through real records for a name I "read" in a trance! Could Marian Kimmer see what a fake I was? Behind those polished lenses did her eyes see right through my claim to be hunting for an ancestor? Had she noted me in her steno book as this week's nut case? No, she was too busy for that. She had real work to do.

And then I saw *Grace* with four entries:

Grace, B.

Grace, J.

Grace, M.

Grace, S.

Shivers spilled over me. Grace, J.! There she was! There I was! No, wait a minute. You don't know this is Jane. It could be James, Jacob, Juba . . . but my Lord, here it was, and it could be Jane. What were the odds of my finding that very name?

I scanned the page for other information but there were only numbers out beside each entry. How frustrating! Was this some kind of code? No, of course not. It was an index. Marian could tell me what it referred to.

But when I got to her desk, I found a note written on her propped-up steno book: "I'm in a meeting across the hall. Knock if there's an emergency."

Emergency? I had to leave town in – I checked my-watch – forty-five minutes. I wouldn't be back till heaven knew when, and this was really important to me. But to Marian? To the city fathers or whatever group she was meet-ing with? A genealogical emergency? I didn't think so. I copied all the information down, gathered my things, and went out into sunshine so bright it stung my eyes.

The records office faces Pulteney Square, so I crossed the street and walked the diagonal path to the fountain, passing beneath maples in their full summer glory. When I came to the blue pool, I sat on its low rim, trailing my hand in warm water. I wanted to feel some connection, not just with Jane Grace, but with myself, the five-year-old who ran here so freely. But I felt only the water on my hand. If I had been Catholic, I would have crossed myself with it.

Instead, I stood up, wiped my hand off on my khaki pants and headed out of the park, down Morris Street to St. Mary's.

It wasn't Sunday this time and, to my great disappointment, the church door was locked. I knocked. Nobody came. I just stood there, as I had at Marian's desk, giving reality a few minutes to change. This time it did. As I walked away, a painter on a ladder at the side of the church called to me, "They keep that locked, but you can get in through the back."

"Oh, thanks!" I said, squinting up at this young guy in cutoffs and a purple tank top.

"Just go around me and in through the day care center door. At the end of the hall, turn right. You'll see a sign to the sanctuary."

"Thank you so much!" I called back, hurrying past him.

As I slipped in the blue metal door, I expected to be stopped and questioned by a day care worker, but nobody appeared. It was very quiet: naptime, maybe. Or maybe they'd gone on a field trip.

The back door to the sanctuary opened and I found my-self in dim light, beside an altar to a little-used saint. None of the candles beneath him were burning anyway. But maybe that was because a stack of lumber had been piled right at his feet. Evidently the exterior painting was only part of St. Mary's summer project. The aisle where I had sobbed the fall before was loaded with pvc pipe. Not only was there no Mass in progress now, but with construction supplies everywhere, it didn't feel like a church at all. Nevertheless, I walked halfway up the aisle and slid into a pew. Just sitting there didn't feel right, so I knelt. Buckets of spackling compound flanked the altar rail. I put my face in my hands.

When I did that, a fist of sorrow pushed so hard against my throat that I almost cried out. With no one around, I let the tears come fast and hard like a summer storm. This time they brought words: *Stay here.*

So I did. I stayed there on my knees for twenty minutes hoping for more words. None came. But as soon as I started to get up, I heard again an inner voice, like a hand on my shoulder commanding: *Stay here!*

I can't stay any longer, I said to Jane in my heart. I have to meet my family. I have to drive on for a job. But I'll come back. I know you were here. I know your name now. I'm going to find somebody to help me find you – I promise!

Still I felt a weight dragging me back as I got to my feet and made my way down the side aisle and past – oh, I could see now, it was St. Joseph, with the toddler Jesus in his arms. The baby was waving. I waved back. Knowing I was late, I ran past the day care, scrambled around the painter on his ladder, and rushed toward the park. Joey and Steve were waiting, hungry. I climbed back into the van, into my life.

8

When we returned from all our travels, there were family birthdays to celebrate, the jungle of the yard to tame, the beginning of school to prepare for. It was September before I called the library in Bath and asked to speak to someone who did local genealogy.

"We have Nikki Brower, a volunteer," the librarian told me, "but she's only here Tuesday and Thursday afternoons."

I called back on schedule. It was easier now that I had a name and date to offer, and I could tell after just a few minutes that Nikki would be good to work with. She wrote down the particulars and said she'd call as soon as she found anything.

"How do I go about paying you?" I asked.

"You don't need to," Nikki said. "It's a library service."

"But what about phone calls?"

"I'll call and let you call me back," she explained. "And if we get into lots of copying, I'll send you a bill."

"This is wonderful!" I said.

She laughed. "People treat you like a queen if you can

help them find their families. I have to warn you, though. It won't be fast. I've got a list of requests ahead of yours, and I only work part-time."

"That's fine," I assured her. "I've got other work too."

CR

Still it was a long three weeks until she called. And then her message was unsettling.

"Mrs. Lyon," she began – nobody calls me Mrs. Lyon except solicitors and school officials – "this is Nikki Brower. I've found Jane Grace –"

"Yes!" I exclaimed, feeling as if I was all at once standing in bright sun.

"Hold on. I'm afraid she can't be the person you're looking for."

Then the shadow passed over. "Why not?"

"This woman can't have been a schoolteacher. She was black, illiterate. She worked as a servant."

I let out my breath. Now what? To come so close and then hit a wall. There must be something, some other way. "Can you find out who she worked for?" I asked. "Maybe there's some family connection." That sounded lame, but I didn't know what else to say. I didn't want her to give up.

"I'll try," Nikki promised.

"Thank you," I said. Then added, "Oh, I didn't call you back!"

"Next time," she said.

Waiting for the next time, I kept fighting off my doubts. Part of me was thinking, 'You got a name. You found a match. That's amazing, but it's not her. The whole thing is just a wild coincidence. You gave it a try. Now let it go.'

But another part – the inside, feeling part – said, 'Just keep looking. You promised.'

Nikki Brower didn't call this time. She wrote:

Dear Mrs. Lyon,

My research shows that Jane Grace worked for the Teeple family. Most likely she had been a slave and stayed on after Emancipation. (I can check this later.) George Teeple ran a lumber business, and he and his wife Lucy had several children, including Ruth who, in the 1860 and 1870 census, is listed as unmarried and living at home. Occupation: schoolteacher. In the 1880 census Ruth does not appear.

I don't know what to make of this.

Let me know if you want anything further.

All best,
Nikki Brower

I went cold all at once. Then hot. Then I started jumping up and down. 'My Lord,' I thought, 'it's really her! Jane had said her mother's name was Lucy. And the lumber business – that would account for the machines she said her father worked with. And as for disappearing, I know what happened to her. She got pregnant. She moved to Wales.' I was crying now, sitting at my desk in my little writing room under the eaves. Who would believe this – right here, in my hand, the evidence, the record of what I'd remembered? But why didn't the boat ticket or passport I'd unwrapped and read in the session with Laura say *Ruth Teeple*?

I thought and thought about this, but I couldn't come up with an answer. Then I tried another approach. I imagined myself as Ruth. Why would I change my name? Well, I wanted a smooth getaway. If I made the arrangements in my own name, I might be followed, caught. And Jane Grace's name was there for the taking. A former slave, she wouldn't have had a birth certificate. But why would I take her name instead of making one up? Because it was the one lasting thing from home I could take with me – the name of this woman who had taken care of me all my life.

So, with the dip of a nib in ink, *Ruth Teeple* became *Jane Grace*.

9

Being a musician, my husband works and sleeps late. Usually I wait till he's up and has had his coffee to begin any conversation, but after I read Nikki's letter, I woke him.

"You won't believe this!" I said. "Nikki found her – Jane Grace – only her name is Ruth Teeple. The census says she's a schoolteacher but then she disappears, so you see . . . ." But of course he didn't see. He wakes up slowly and could barely see me. I apologized for bothering him and called Ann.

"All right!" she said after I'd blurted out my news. "Isn't that amazing? You think that could really be her?"

I babbled on.

"Slow down and tell me again," Ann said.

This was helpful. I could picture Ann in her little hand-made farmhouse out on Mauk Ridge with the yellow sticker on the refrigerator proclaiming, "I'm a Quaker. In case of emergency, please be quiet." It was steadying. I took a deep breath and went back through my revelations.

"Very good," Ann said at the end. "What will you do now?"

I laughed. "I don't know," I said. "I haven't thought farther."

"Can you find out where they lived?" Ann asked. "Or where she taught? That might lead to something."

"Good idea," I said. "I'll ask Nikki."

Getting ready to call her that afternoon, I felt a little fragile. When telling Ann – or even groggy Steve – that Ruth had taken Jane's name, I felt confident that it was true. I just knew somehow. But telling Nikki, whose job was not just connecting dots but searching out the dots to connect, I felt shaky. Had I just made up this dot because I wanted to? Was I filing down a puzzle piece to make it fit?

Jane hadn't admitted changing her name in the past-life session, but then she hadn't admitted being pregnant either. Secrecy had been her life, after its turning point, and this story felt right to me. I decided to accept it, unless something else came along to persuade me otherwise.

So I called Nikki and told her what I thought.

"Hmmmm," she said. "I'd like to see that document with her name. Do you still have it?"

"No," I said nervously. I should have seen this coming.

"Well, is it still in your family?"

"I don't think so."

"Where did you see it?"

'Oh Lord,' I thought, 'if I tell her where I saw it, she's going to think I'm a total flake and hang up.'

"Look, Nikki, " I began, "it's complicated. And I've got to take my son to his violin lesson in a few minutes. What if I write you about the history and then we talk again?"

"Sure," she said. "That's fine." Did she sound peeved behind these mild words? Was she thinking I shouldn't have called her if I didn't have time to talk? Probably not. Probably it was just my unease I was sensing. I thanked her and hung up.

That night, pen clenched, I wrote a very brief account of my search – how it started and where it had taken me thus far. If she thought me too weird to work with, so be it. She'd already helped me. And it was better to be honest. I hadn't lied to her yet; I'd only left out a crucial part. The way Jane did. Now I put it in.

Much to my relief, Nikki was game to keep going. She wrote back:

> I'm not sure what you're doing but that's up to you.
>
> I am interested in where you're going, if you want to send more of your tale. I'm not sure what I've found fits what you are doing; or if what I'm sending you fits.
>
> It interests me to "dig up" information about a family and their place in the community . . . .

Nikki's calm words were like a hand on my shoulder. Even knowing the nature of the journey, she was willing to be a guide. Someone beyond my own circle trusted what I was doing. I could tell the truth. I was less alone.

10

At one point in this writing I thought it would be helpful to read through journals and create a timeline of my search for Jane Grace. However, when I went to the shelves, I saw there are over forty just since 1997.

That's part of what makes this so dizzying: I'm reaching not only for Jane's nineteenth-century story and my nineteen-fifties one, but back through nine very full years of my present life. In that period, my older son made his way to independence and my younger son grew from a fifth grader to a senior in high school. My marriage hit rough water twice and came through to smoother parts of the stream. I wrote – or completed and published – fourteen books, spoke in over two hundred schools. Cheered at baseball games, hosted sleepovers, sang at Easter vigils, spent a year or so at the grocery or cooking or bowing before the washer and the dryer. Who could go back through all that life? Especially when it's rushing forward at the same heedless speed? Life never waits for us to catch up, sort it out, put it in perspective. With each breath in, it gives us the future. With each breath out, it takes us farther from the past.

So I will go on imperfectly, with what I remember. I will hold memory's shape-shifting hand.

I did look at my journal from the summer of Nikki's letter, though. It shows that on August 6th I turned to Jane herself for understanding, asking this other part of me, whether remembered or intuited or imagined, "Do you have a voice? Do you want to tell me something?" Here is her reply:

The house is gone, my father's house. The family's gone. There is no one to receive me. You can do that. You are doing that. And believing me despite a few difficulties. I need to be received, believed. I need family. Even a momentary five-year-old will do. Just follow the thread and tell my story. It's not for me to tell you what you'll find.

I must add, don't expect anyone to make this easy.

Other doors I knocked on were sealed tight. I spent the second half of my life locked out. Granted, I'm the one who left, who shut the door. I didn't think I turned the key, though.

I thought I had it with me – or more foolish still, I thought I wouldn't need one. And part of me has been wandering ever since, body or no body. If you could just find me a place to rest. Go back with me. You're small. You could crawl through a basement window. Never mind if the house is gone. Do you see me? Well then.

You could crawl through that window, the one Father never locked, swim through dirt and cobwebs, come up the bare stairs. At the top you might want to take off your shoes and carry them. Mother always had us do that. For the carpet.

Pull open the door, turn to your left, come through the narrow passage into the wide hall. There's the door ahead, see it? There's a key on the window ledge of the sidelight. A key on edge. Now. You've got it. I see you through the glass. Let me in.

So that's what she wanted: to come home, to bring her life full circle. To be received. And I was the receiver.

I could do that. I've done that with lots of voices, lots of characters. I write fiction, after all. But I'd never done it in this fashion. Never with someone who showed up in my life. Whose name was in the census, whose footsteps might be traced, whose grave lay somewhere. And I didn't go after this story. It came after me.

11

There was more doubt here than I can put into the telling. More time spent being lost. Jane said to follow the thread, but often I didn't feel as if I had one. A snippet of embroidery, maybe. A froth of tatting on a pillowslip. But nothing to get me through the labyrinth. However, whenever I was just about to give up, I would catch a glimpse, a slither of something pulled along ahead.

It happened in one of the last past-life sessions when Laura asked Jane if there were any magazines or newspapers in her Welsh classroom.

"A newspaper, yes," she said.

"What is it?" Laura asked.

"*The Standard*," Jane replied.

"Is that all?"

"It's from Bristol, I think," Jane replied.

"Pick it up," Laura insisted. "Can you see a date?"

And there I stand, as Jane, in my long fawn-colored skirt. I see the ivory sleeves of my blouse and my small hands holding the paper with its heavy gothic type. My eyes strain to see the date, blurred a little on the grainy page. "1896?" I offer. "No, 1846."

"Can you read any headlines?" Laura asks, but the scene disappears like a fade-out in a movie.

I saw those hands, though. I felt my life inside them. And they were not the long, slender, round-nailed hands I have now. The nails crowning each short finger were tapered and the nailbeds more ivory than pink. I don't have the gold filigree ring she wore on her little finger either.

When the session was over, Laura and I discussed the date.

"It doesn't make sense," I protested. "She wasn't even there in 1846. She didn't arrive till the mid-seventies."

"They must have kept it for some reason then," Laura speculated. "Maybe you can find out."

Yeah, right, I thought, suddenly back in my cynic-skeptic mode. It felt like it does when your shower goes cold because somebody flushed the toilet. *The Bristol Standard* probably doesn't even exist, I thought. And even if it does, who would go chasing a phantom edition which has the wrong date for a person with a false identity to be reading in a country I can't prove she ever even went to?

Me, as it turns out.

I couldn't resist the date, that little glimpse of fuzzy, ink-black thread. I called the reference desk at the University of Kentucky library. "Had there ever been such a newspaper?" I wanted to know. The guy working the desk said he would check and call back.

He did, in less than an hour. Yes, there had been a *Bristol Standard*. It ceased publication in 1850.

My God. "Thank you," I said. "Is there any way I can look at issues from, say, 1846?"

"Not here," he said. "At the British Library, probably. Or maybe one in Bristol. Perhaps you could order copies."

"I'll look into that," I told him. "Thanks again." I hung up, exhilarated and dumbfounded. What was I supposed to do now?

Even if I located a source for copies of the paper, I didn't know when in 1846 I was looking for. And even if it was a weekly – I forgot to ask about that – I couldn't order fifty-two copies. How would I ever get the right one?

I let these questions simmer and did what I could do. I went to the library for books on Welsh history. Something momentous must have happened in 1846.

12

When I got my borrowed history home, I sat in my grandmother's chair sipping tea and reading about labor unrest in the coal- and iron-producing towns of Wales in the 1830's. Poor housing, inflated prices at the company store, owners living in luxury earned by the workers' struggle – it all sounded familiar to someone from eastern Kentucky, where a similar story was acted out a hundred years later.

Then I paged through *Language, Ethnicity, and Education* where Bud Khleif explains that, in 1846, William Williams, an MP from Coventry "moved that an inquiry be conducted into the state of education in [Wales]." An all-English commission spent six months studying Welsh schools and concluded that Welsh itself was the source of all the problems, "'a vast drawback to Wales and a manifold barrier to the moral progress and commercial prosperity of the people.'" As if that wasn't enough, the commission condemned Welsh character too. Clearly inferior to the English, the Welsh were labeled dirty, intemperate liars with no sense of justice or sexual restraint. The best way to remedy this situation was "'to get rid of their language.'"

So in 1870 Parilament passed the Education Act making English the language of instruction in all British elementary schools. No wonder a classroom in Wales kept this news from 1846. Williams' motion led to the condemnation of Welsh language. It also gave Jane Grace her job. What I do wonder at is how this history connects with the crusading side of my own life.

As a writer and teacher from the Appalachian coalfields, I have traipsed from elementary school to church basement, from college auditorium to bowling alley proclaiming the richness of mountain language and culture. I've led workshops introducing teachers and students to writers who speak from our common ground.

Often I give a talk called "Voiceplace" which closes with words from Irish poet, Seamus Heaney, "A poet has to find the language that makes the common, almost unconscious life vocal; he must be a voice box for something that is in the land, the people." I go on to say:

> *You can't be a voicebox for your own feelings and experiences, much less for your place, if you've been taught that your first speech was wrong. If you abandon or ridicule your voiceplace, you forfeit a deep spiritual connection.*

Teaching in Wales (*Cymru* is its native name), Jane would have witnessed firsthand the effect on children of having their language condemned and taken away. She would have seen what it cost the community. By law, she had to displace her students, teaching them in a foreign tongue. In this system, learning cut them off from the emotional foundation of home words, from their parents and their history, too.

In a curious way Jane and her students were in the same boat. She was displaced, newly named, with an ocean between her and all that had been her life. It's as if wrenching circumstances crafted them, teacher and students, for each other.

And I have to ask, looking at the role of all these forces in Jane's life: did they craft me, too, who took my crusade for mountain voices on the road a century after she arrived in Cymru?

13

Any story is infinite. That's what I'm beginning to see. The process of writing is one of wrestling with that infinite angel to claim some finite strand to tell. You cannot tell one one-thousandth of it all. And if you could, parts of the telling would contradict other parts.

When Joey, my younger son, was about three, he picked up a piece of paper and said, "I will read you a story." I can still see him, standing on plump bare feet in front of me, the bottom snap of his blue p.j. top undone so that a bit of his round belly was visible. He held the paper in front of him like a book and proclaimed, "Actually. Then. So. The end!" I laughed and clapped, amazed. All day his words came back to me. That is story, I thought. He got the essence. *Actually* is what we're given at the beginning, the problem, the longing. *Then* is the quest, its obstacles and turning. *So* is where we end up.

Now I realize that this pattern is a way of telling story, but it's not the reality of story as we experience it. Life is Actually. Then. Actually. So. So what then? Actually:

Opposite Actually. Then, Then, So, Actually. Actually x Actually. Actually + someone's memory of Then - So. So divided by So. So-So. Not actually. Are you kidding? Who says? Now, then, actually . . .

I didn't know this multiplicity when I began my journey. I wanted to find out whose memory I'd tapped into, research her story, and see if there was something she wanted from me. If someone calls and leaves a message to call back, you want to know why. You punch in the number. In my case, getting a number was lengthy and complicated, but the principle is the same. She called when I was five. Forty years later I began to try to call back.

Do you understand how cell phones work? Can you explain the mechanics beyond, "Well, there's a satellite and towers, a signal and numbers . . . ."? Probably not. For most of us, this is true of major things we work with every day. The computer, for example. The internal combustion engine. Okay, some of you know about that. If so, think of something more challenging. Like our brains. Our hearts. They use electrical impulses, yes. But do you really understand that? The quantum mechanics underneath it?

If you are the rare reader who does, you'll know that when you get to subatomic particles, you have arrived, not at the answers Newtonian science taught us to expect, but at questions, contradictions, mystery. How do two particles communicate instantaneously with no means, no medium between them? We don't know, folks. Ultimately, we don't know how the lily blooms, why we hiccup, or the route of miracle my hand expresses as a crochet of words, in metallic blue gel, on this page.

So, if at the level of our infinitesimal invisibleness we are multiple and contradictory, how could our stories, our enormous selves, be otherwise? And perhaps, as size increases, we become more wildly, more dramatically so.

Then.

Actually.

14

Given this, when I tell you what happened next, I trust you will not falter. I phoned first the British and then the Bristol libraries, only to learn that the *Standard* ceased publication in 1843. Not only was Jane not there to read it in 1846, it didn't exist! I was hugely disappointed to learn this. I sat at my desk in my writing room, the low ceiling painted a pale pink called Bath Salt in honor of this search, and I felt robbed. This connection had meant so much and now it wasn't even true! Oh, this whole thing was absurd, ridiculous, one long delusion . . . . I just needed to give it up.

By now I was familiar with this Dance of Doubt. While I couldn't choose to sit it out, I could put less energy into it. And when it wound down, what I saw was this:

The connection between Jane's life and mine which the *Standard* led me to – the Welsh and Appalachian struggle for voice and self – was no less luminous to me because the newspaper wasn't published that year. If the student working the reference desk that day hadn't made a mistake and read me the wrong dates, I wouldn't have found this deeper correspondence. It was more gift than error, what he gave me. And as a friend of mine, herself a librarian, pointed out, the *Standard* could refer to the dominant view of the time, the prevailing ideology, and Bristol, though separated from Wales by only the Severn, was irreparably English. The MP for Coventry certainly proclaimed a standard in 1846, and by the 1870's everyone in Wales, including my Jane, was going to be held to it.

As I write this, I see that the date is like her name, too, presented and then taken back. I found it in the record, yes, but then it didn't mean what I thought. This overall pattern must have something to teach me. On some level, I am a student of this story. As we say in the mountains, I am going to school to Jane Grace.

About the same time the *Standard* fell through, I learned that Nikki, my link with Bath history, was moving. To Bethlehem (Pennsylvania) at Christmas. If she could find someone else to work with me, she would, but for the rest of the year she would be too busy sorting, packing, and getting two houses on the market to be of use. Another set-back. A delay. What could I do?

First, I could continue what I'd already begun, writing to Welsh archives to try to trace Jane's story there. Not much material was online at this point, so letters, actual paper packets of words, had to cross the Atlantic twice for each inquiry. The second thing I could do was keep trying to write in her voice.

So here is another doubleness: as I searched for her story in the world of weight and number, of fading script and microfiche at the Mormon Family History Center, I also searched artistically, by way of imagination, listening for what she might say.

Where does a writer go in this listening? Into memory? Her unconscious? The collective unconscious, a sort of story table that runs beneath our individual lives like the water table beneath the ground we walk on? This travel to the word-place is my constant journey, but I can't tell you how it works. I've published six novels, and it still feels like a miracle to me.

In the last stages of revising my novel *With a Hammer for My Heart*, which came soon after my first trip to Bath, I spent a day reading case studies at a Veteran's hospital. Garland, one of my main characters, was a World War II vet living out his demons. While I'd done a lot of reading about the war and post-traumatic stress, I hadn't looked at actual testimonies because I was afraid that seeing the real thing would overpower my narrative. With the book almost finished, I wanted to read them so that if Garland's way of living and voicing his pain were unbelievable, I could change them.

In a dusty beige cinderblock office with windows like metal ice trays, a clerk handed me a stack of file folders soft with use. I held my breath. She was putting people's lives in my hands. These were sacred pages. And the voices they held might make my own pages fall apart. For Garland, and for the integrity of the novel, I was about to face, straight-on, the inadequacy of my imagination.

I was trembling. What did I know about war? Books and movies? What did they mean? During Vietnam, my husband was a C. O. and my brother had a college deferment. In World War II, my father enlisted and was then discharged due to arthritis of the spine, and my grandfathers were cutting timber and building coal camps during World War I. I heard no war stories growing up. I realize that's often true of kids whose dads went to war, too, but their families feel its blunt impact, the profundity of what cannot be said. I didn't have that. I had no qualifications for writing Garland except the storyteller's openness to receive, to be what Lewis Hyde calls "that begging bowl to which the gift is drawn."

And as I sat reading in the corner room of the old brick hospital on shady ground off Leestown Road, voice after voice, story after story, said that Garland could have been there. He *was* there, under other names, with other particulars. His tortured memory which released its force in violence against those he loved, his elaborate self-hatred and concealment, his certainty that his actions as a soldier – in our name – were unspeakable. Who could bear it? Who would want to know? And what can't be spoken can never be forgiven. Thus the person is trapped forever in the horror of his story.

Seeing this, I sat in that airless room overcome by these soldiers' words and by the fact that Garland gave his to me. How could that be?

I had to live with this experience a while before I knew what to make of it, but finally here is what came to me: I listened. Garland talked. The dowser doesn't create water. By a certain attunement and concentration, she locates where to dig and the stream bubbles up. When the water is a voice, the stream may ebb and flow. Sometimes it may bring up underground trash that renders it unfit to drink. But flow it will. Garland's voice had. Jane's would. I had to seek out places – outer and inner – where her voice would come to the surface. Amid all my research I had to make room to receive.

73

When I asked why she came to me, this was her answer:

I had a secret
I needed to tell
You had a voice

I had a heart
exiled, broken

I needed
your breath
to cry
your shadow
to cast
your hand
to reach
for the door
I had closed
your fingers
to feel for
the pulse of
my story
your lips
to speak my
name

15

Nikki did find another genealogist, a woman named Emma Jones. Emma didn't live in Bath, however. Her home was about twenty miles away. Plus she was retired and traveled a lot with her husband. But she was interested and would help when she could. Since Nikki had given her all my material, I didn't have to explain anything. I just went on writing in my voice about the search and in Jane's voice about her life. And I waited.

It was fall, 1997. *With a Hammer for My Heart* had just come out and I was doing some flying trips to promote it. I'm a homebody and I don't like to fly, but it's what the word-road calls for, so I do it. Also that fall I worked in fourteen schools as well as had other one-day jobs. Joey turned eleven. My older son Benn moved out and moved back in. I don't want to give the impression that all I did was sit around watching the mailbox, though I did check it several times a day when I was home.

Waiting for word. It's a lot of what a writer does. Light candles, brew coffee, take a walk, fill your favorite pen with your favorite shade of ink: whatever works. Or has worked. Or might work. It's all so iffy. Once I have a voice I can follow it, but those first sweet words, the scrap of the song of a life, have to come to me. Not just once but every time I sit down. Even with this writing, which doesn't require the breath of a character, I still have to hear the melody, still have to feel something tug me onward. Otherwise, dear reader, the trail gives out. I would find myself in thickets where you would never follow.

CR

Once I let myself write for Jane, I found she had a great deal to say. Some of it came from the past-life sessions, just telling the same events more fully. Other parts filled in the blanks or added elements which were entirely new. And as the story emerged, through the fall of 1997 and the winter of 1998, I began to try to put a book together.

I wasn't sure about publishing this story. I could imagine many ways reviewers could tear it apart. I could do that myself. But writing books is what writers do. It's how we live and breathe and support ourselves. We are always looking for books. And in this case, whatever my qualms, I felt called to bear witness.

The result, finished during a snowstorm while my husband was gone to Callifornia on business, was a fairly lumpy three-part manuscript: my childhood experience, the research (conventional and otherwise), and Jane's story. I know now that it was much too early for me to "finish" this project. I still had a lot of work ahead. But I needed the milestone of a first draft, and two mysterious things happened in the process of reaching it.

Before the snowstorm hit, I had gone through clothes of Benn's that I had saved for Joey, weeding out ones that were way out of style or the right size but the wrong season. Joey had sorted through his closet, too, and together we had filled two black trash bags with jeans and tee shirts, pullovers and sweat pants to hand on to Goodwill. I'd carried the bags to the van, meaning to drop them off the next day. Then came the snow and there they sat, waiting for clear roads.

On the day I'd printed half of the manuscript, I got a call from a local charity after supper. They would have a truck in my neighborhood the next day. Yes, they knew the roads were bad, but with this weather, people were in need of warm clothes, and conditions were supposed to get better overnight. So I promised a donation, put on coat and boots, and crunched down the path I'd shoveled to the van. Unlocking the back hatch, I lifted it and saw not only the two bags I'd heaved in there days before but a third, smaller bag. Could Steve have thrown it in before he left and I just hadn't noticed? I mused on the possibility as I wrestled the bags back up the glistening steps and into the house.

In the living room I checked the ones I'd filled just to make sure everything was in order, and then I opened the third one. Wait a minute! Still in my coat, I sat on the couch and took the items out one by one: a little girl's red corduroy jumper and white shirt with matching red trim, pale blue pants and a blue polo shirt, yellow leggings and a tunic which had an appliqued house with a soft plastic door that opened. My God! Where did they come from? I began to shake. I didn't have a little girl. I didn't have friends with little girls that age. No neighbors either. And anyway, even if I had, what would their clothes be doing in my van? I didn't put them there. Steve was out of town. The van was locked. People don't break into vehicles in snowstorms to leave old clothes inside.

Okay, they weren't old. They looked used but still had some wear in them. And they'd been recently washed – I could smell the fabric softener – and neatly folded. Folded with memories, I imagined, as Benn's and Joey's had been, ready to be passed on with tears and blessings.

To me?? What was I doing with these clothes, which would have fit me on my first trip to Bath?

Feeling scared and a little angry that somebody was playing a trick on me, I called Joey up from the family room in the basement where he was watching TV. I showed him the outfits, five or six in all, laid out on the green couch.

"Can you tell me what these are?" I asked.

He raised his eyebrows at me. "Uh, Mom," he began, "they're, like, kid's clothes. A little girl's. Used. What are you doing with them?"

"Exactly. I mean, I don't know. They were in the van." And I explained the scenario to him. He hadn't put them there, he said, with a twelve-year old's instinctive don't-blame-me tone. Well, of course not. I didn't think so. The truth was I just wanted him to confirm their reality. To make sure I wasn't dreaming.

"Ask Dad," Joey said, which I did on the phone later that night. But Steve had no clue either.

Those clothes gave me the authentic creeps. Unwilling to touch them after I talked with Steve, I left the stacks on the couch all night like I was packing some phantom child's suit-case.

By morning the roads had improved and school re-opened. As soon as Joey was off, I put the clothes back in the bag. I still felt unnerved and couldn't wait to get the clothes out on the porch for pick up. I was too freaked out to think of taking a picture of them, and I certainly wasn't going to keep any.

Now I wish I had. I wish I'd kept the tunic with its house and the door like the one Jane had asked me to open.

16

Not that I think Jane Grace put those clothes in my van. I have no idea how they got there. Neither does anyone else who had anything to do with the van. But I do think their being there is part of this pattern, this story. Scientists now accept the fact that the observer influences the experiment. We don't stand separate from objective data. Everything connects and interacts. So perhaps looking for pattern creates pattern; the energy of the search calls out what will be found.

Some sort of energy affected what happened after the Cedar Lakes Lodge truck had carted off my three bags full. Focused again on the manuscript I hit a printing snag. No matter what command I gave the computer, the printer would not give forth Jane's account of the voyage to Wales, her delight in her baby growing inside and in the colors of the sea.

Rather than strike the contraption with a large stick, I decided to switch tactics and folders and print a section in my voice which I'd revised that morning. After the necessary clicks and keystrokes, the printer started humming and laying letters on the page. What a relief! This was no time for a systems breakdown.

Then I looked at the page emerging like a squared-off tongue from the printer's mouth. Was part of it blue? I got up from my desk and stood watching. Here is what I saw: the computer merged our voices, which I had been keeping so carefully apart. It doubled Jane's voice and made certain lines larger, like the Oversoul's voice over all. It split the word VOYAGE down the middle and reversed its halves, setting them down on opposite sides of the ocean of the page. Like her journey and mine. And it printed, in the breathing spaces between paragraphs:

the deep blue sea

able to keep that vow

clear, ornamented

belonged to, s/he probably went to church and, at the very least, I might run

into a local historian after the services.

First, came the 8 a.m. Eucharist at St. Thomas Episcopal. I almost

My memory of the voyage is lit by the overhead lamp swaying, pitching

in the opposite direction from the ship. The swing of light and shadow added

to my queasiness, but I was never sick. A mercy. As I held on tight in my

berth in the night, I told the baby, "You have got the ocean for your cradle,

little one. The deep blue sea."

And it did look blue by moments. But it could show a hundred other

colors as well: emerald, olive, silver, gun gray, black. I have seen water coral

pink at sunrise shine orange and purple at day's end. Old gold, turquoise,

lightning white -- all are tricks light plays on water. The voyage taught me

this.

And I thought how strange it is, how false, that when we teach children

colors, we name red, blue, green. We do not say these are categories of

color, each the lid to a marvelous paintbox. We might as well teach them

only bird, and count it sufficient for warbler, phoenix, finch. My child shall

know better, I vowed. My students shall not be so blind. With my students I

have been able to keep that vow.

But my companion of the voyage, she who danced across the ocean,

was to see nothing. Not long after ship and train carried us to Wales, pain

brought her to the shore of this world. But she would not cross over. The

doctor wrote in a clear, ornamented hand

S.S. _____ LUCY GRACE   STILLBORN

She was so full of motion! How could she be still?

Was it on the roll of the ocean, in some blissful swim, that the cord

wrapped around her neck? Did it lie there like a necklace until birth slid it

As I confessed, I don't understand how the computer works, but it seems plausible to me that part of one unprinted file could be stuck in memory and somehow get released when another file was called on. But how another, larger version of File One could be printed over top of them both in the very color the words are naming I cannot fathom.

I know this means something. I know from the sense of awe and connection I felt as I read it for the first time. But I don't have words for what it means. I can't label it, make it explicit. The page is like a window to Jane, though. I can almost see her.

THROUGH

If the weft of space-time is warped with holes
like the rose trellis in my grandmother's yard,
can I look through one diamond window and see
your garden? See you older now, bent and thickened,
breaking off dill and nasturtiums for your salad,
weeding forget-me-knots? I feel the strain in the arc
of your back, the chill through your thick sweater.
In my hand, the pen. In yours, green stems.
Zest from ink on this page.

17

In addition to my historical research, I did a lot of reading about reincarnation, psychic ability, and quantum physics. I wanted to see how other cultures experience and explain reincarnation, what we understand about paranormal ways of knowing, and what I could grasp of scientific thinking about time, space, and events beyond our notion of causality. All of this informed my thinking, but I have to say that I always had trouble reading unambiguous past-life claims. They seemed reductive and oversimplified, opening into fewer rather than more dimensions.

One book which investigated paranormal experience recommended a medium in New York City named Jane Grace Kennedy. Though I argued mightily with myself about calling her – surely contacting a medium would squander my last scrap of credibility – ultimately I could not resist her name. I left a message and when she called back, all I told her was that I wanted to contact a person I might have been in a former life, a woman whose name she shared, and who had connected with me as a child.

At first, Jane Kennedy wasn't sure she could do it. "This is not just a person who has died," she said, "but an aspect of your own soul." However, she agreed to try. When she did, the first thing she told me was, "She loves it when you sing to her." And I saw my small self singing in that black Ford as we drove up Highway 17.

CR

Spring passed with no news from Emma, the geneaologist. Summer came and my mother-in-law died of Alzheimer's. She'd been disappearing into it for eight years, her face assuming a hard stare, her quick wit lost in the jumble they call word salad. Still, her death was a shock and a loss, and we arrived at our annual beach week sad and shaken.

One morning as I sat trying to read at the edge of the Atlantic, all I could think of was how the sea of days rushes in and takes what it will and there's nothing we can do about it. Therefore, if we have any urgent business, we'd better do it now. My manuscript was at a standstill. I couldn't wait for other people to keep the process moving. I needed to go deeper, reach another layer of it. I needed to get a grant and follow Jane Grace to Wales.

Part of me was fearful of this, part was scornful. How could you even consider spending time and money – I don't care whose money – going on such a wild goose chase? I asked myself. And suppose you get over there and get lost in this story? Suppose you decide you are Jane Grace and never come back? People do that kind of thing, you know.

I acknowledged that these voices had their wisdom.

From the outside, this would look crazy. But I didn't live from outside. I lived from the inside, from experiencing a story that would not let me go. And if it did turn out to be a wild goose chase, well, it was my wild goose and for some reason I had to go after it. I knew if I did this I'd have to keep myself grounded. I'd have to sound grounded on the grant applications. I'd have to figure out what to do when I got there.

I began to think on that. From places Jane referred to in the past-life session, I knew I wanted to go to Swansea, to other sites in Glamorgan – the southwest county – and to coal country. But that was all. I had no thought of going north.

Then in the middle of our beach week, my sister-in-law Betty and I finished the jigsaw puzzle she'd brought, and I went to the toy chest in our rental house to see if I could find another one.

The Masonite floor of the chest was strewn with kids' puzzles and loose pieces: Garfield, Barney, Thomas the Tank Engine, and so forth. There was only one offering for older puzzlers: a photo of a three-arched stone bridge with a village at one end and a cottage with a roof covered with crimson leaves at the other. I searched the box to see where this lovely place was and read:

Inigo Jones Bridge, North Wales

A wave of chills rolled over my sunburned skin.

"Guess I have to go there," I joked with Steve, showing him the picture and the name.

"Guess so," he said.

"No, really," I said, still smiling. "I mean it."

"I know you do," he answered.

When we finally got the puzzle worked, it was beautiful but was missing five pieces. Me and Jane, I thought. And who else?

CR

Back at home, once school got underway, I began work on applications to the Kentucky Arts Council and the Kentucky Foundation for Women. I already had a manuscript in process, so coming up with a work sample was no problem. The problem was how to describe what I was doing. If I told the truth, would they dismiss my request for funding out of hand? Perhaps with a note saying, "Thank you for letting us review this, but at present we do not fund individual delusions?" (Such a note is not so far-fetched as you might think. A friend of mine swears that when she called her health insurance for referral to a therapist, the interminable option recording said, "If you are hearing voices, press 1. If you are a danger to yourself or others, press 2." "And if you look to these folks for help," my friend said, "you're really crazy.")

I decided to tell the truth. I wouldn't feel right otherwise. And if I got the money, it wouldn't be under false pretenses.

Applications completed, I settled into fall jobs and writing. Emma, back from her summer travels, sent me an obituary for Ruth's brother Solomon and an article confirming the Maypole dances Ruth had described as part of her childhood in the past-life sessions. Interesting but not especially helpful. My Welsh inquiries came up blank, too.

Then my editor asked me to come to New York to speak at the sales conference about an upcoming book. My travel and expenses would be paid. And I would be within a few hours of Bath! I decided to fly up early, rent a car, and spend a couple of days exploring. This time I wouldn't be passing through. I could stay. And I'd be alone. The thought was both exciting and scary. But I told myself, "If you can go to Wales, you can certainly go to Bath. This will be good practice." So off I went.

If you've ever done genealogical research, you know how often you reach your information source only to learn that the courthouse burned soon after the year you're looking for and all the records you want were destroyed. In the South, a variation of this situation is, "Oh honey, that's when the Yankees came through."

In Bath, I determined from an overall employee list that Ruth taught in the Campbell District – Campbell was her mother's maiden name – but an afternoon's search in the basement of the Davenport Library revealed nothing further. There was no explanation of why the records of Ruth's teaching were missing.

Like Lyon, Davenport is a big name in Bath. Founding fathers, early settlers: that story. My brother Robert pointed out the synchronicity of this. *Davenport* was one of his favorite words as a small child. Nobody knew where he'd heard it, but the sound made him happy and he said it over and over. This childhood delight might have been forgotten except that when he was a freshman at Yale, he was assigned to Davenport College. We joked about it again when he married Betty, an Iowa girl, since Davenport was an Iowa city we'd all heard of. It turns out that Davenport, Iowa, was named for the Davenports of Bath. So what?

I don't know. Maybe it's another manifestation of the fractal principle, where the smallest part of a design replicates the whole. *Davenport* is a tiny detail in this story, much smaller than *Lyon*, my name, being the name of the fellowship hall at the Presbyterian Church, which itself is smaller that the elementary school being called Dana Lyon. It seems to me that *Lyon* is like an echo of the main theme and *Davenport* more like an overtone. But I don't know. For that matter, throughout my life, I've had major figures named Ruth and Jane. Friends and teachers, including Ruth Stone who taught the graduate poetry workshop at Indiana University and changed my life.

I haven't mentioned this because it's *too much*, like trying to name every tree you can see before you take another step in the woods. I acknowledge it now just to say that the big coincidences, synchronicities — whatever you want to call them — of this story are not singular but part of a web of connection. To ennumerate all the small correspondences I found would overwhelm this narrative. As far as I can tell, this is the way the world is made. I just see it because I've been alerted to it and am paying attention. Or perhaps there is more synchronicity in my life because I am looking. I just know it's there. In spades. And I feel sure that if you want to look, you'll find it's in your life too.

18

That first night, I stayed in a motel which looked fine in the brochure I'd gotten from the Chamber of Commerce but in fact was just over the line between plain and seedy. Chipped bed, stuttering lamp, no in-room phone. (And I didn't have a cell phone.) It was after dark when I got there, so I didn't leave in search of somewhere else, but disturbing dreams woke me through the night, and the next morning, from the pay phone on the light pole by the highway, I called the Days Inn. Lesson learned: check it out before you check in. Sometimes local color is mud.

Cars sped past on this clear December morning. In the distance, the northern Appalachian mountains looked soft, like tabby cats bunched up on the horizon. Chilled, I drove toward town and had eggs and bacon in a small, thick-mug diner. Then I headed for Campbell, a nearby town where records say Ruth Teeple taught. En route, I got sidetracked by a cemetery.

Unlike eastern Kentucky, western New York has great stretches of flat land. Folks there live beside mountains, not between them. So Hope Cemetery stands completely level and open beneath great oak trees. It's more like a park interrupted by gravestones than the rolling, catalpa-edged Resthaven where my father and grandparents are buried.

Hope was empty at this hour, except for two men, one operating a ditch witch, the other standing alongside in a red hooded sweat shirt, guiding the digging of a grave.

At first I wandered. It wasn't a huge cemetery, though considerably more populous than Campbell itself. I decided to go row by row. If the Teeples were here, I'd find them.

This shouldn't have taken long, but you know how it is with gravestones. Without intent you find yourself bending over, peering at lichened letters, imagining once-vivid lives. Maybe this is our instinctive bowing to the dead, our acknowledging that they too walked here just as we shall lie with them. Not surprisingly, I found Lyons buried there, but I found Fowlers as well, *Fowler* being my mother's maiden name and that of a street in Bath. The white winter sun was considerably higher in the sky when, about three-fourths of the way through, I came to a pair of gray arched stones for George and Lucy Teeple. George's marker had been broken off and restored, the jagged split still evident. No flowers, but a little flag stood between the graves, probably set out on Veteran's Day just a few weeks before. *Had George fought in the Civil War?* I wrote this question in my pocket notebook. I also took a picture of their stones, along with those of their sons, Joshua and Solomon, buried by wives, Catherine and Huldah.

My weight was already in my heel to turn away when a much smaller russet stone, some distance to the left of Lucy's, caught my eye. Stepping close I saw that it wasn't a worked stone at all, although it was set on its edge into the sod, obviously a marker. Irregular, brown and gray, naked of speech as God made it.

Have you ever been searching for one thing and found something else, something you didn't even know you were looking for? Some part of me recognized this stone, was pulled back by the weight of it. With a lurch of my heart I knew I was standing at the grave of the real Jane Grace.

For most of her life, according to U.S. law, she had "belonged" to Lucy Campbell, who received her as a gift when they were both four. I knew this from records Nikki had sent. Even after Emancipation, she had stayed on with Lucy. And here she lay now, too much an intimate to be buried elsewhere, too invisible to have a name. Anyway, Ruth took it.

Realizing this brought a swing of vertigo, as if someone had turned the dial of the world forty-five degrees to the left. The ground seemed to rise beneath my right foot, and the only way I kept myself from falling over or throwing up was by focusing on that wordless stone. It anchored me till the wave of dizzyness passed.

I wasn't supposed to know whose grave this was. Only the Teeples, who had 'owned' Jane Grace, would have known, when they visited, who lay beneath that stone. Her name, the very fact of her existence, would have died with them. But it didn't. Because of that trip up highway 17 when I was five, I knew. I was her witness.

19

Leaving Hope, I drove back to Bath and parked in front of the Dana Lyon School. The Historical Walking Tour brochure informed me that it was a descendant of the Haverling School, established in 1849, and though I had found nothing to indicate that Ruth ever taught there, I thought the library might have old yearbooks from surrounding schools as well. It would be so wonderful to have a photograph.

Carrying one of my picture books as introduction and gift, I stepped through the front door and into the office right next to it. The school secretary, clad in a red and green Christmas sweater that jingled as she walked, listened to my request and said she was sure a visit would be fine, but she had to get the principal's okay.

I sat in a plastic chair, next to a little boy who'd gotten a nosebleed in gym.

"Are you waiting for the nurse?" I asked him.

"Hunh-uh," he said. "The nurse is sick. My mom's coming to get me."

"Good," I said, hit with a sudden ache because here I

was two days' drive away and what if Joey had a nosebleed? The long reach of instinct and conditioning took hold and shook me good. 'Steve is there,' I insisted to myself. 'He works at home. He could be at school in ten minutes. He's not an uninvolved dad. He knows who the doctor is –'

Jingling interrupted my angst as the secretary called, waving a visitor's pass. "Just go up the front stairs and turn right," she instructed. "You'll see the library at the end of the hall."

"Thanks," I said. And to the little boy, "Hope your mom gets here soon."

I climbed the old stairs with their wrought-iron balustrade and wooden railing, though I wanted to run out the front door, jump into my rental car (a Mirage, of course), and drive straight to Kentucky. 'Stop it,' I told myself. 'He's thirteen. You'll be gone less than a week. You know you have these meltdowns, but you've got to do your work.'

'Work? But I'm not getting paid,' another side of me said. 'It's not like I'm supporting my family. That would be different.'

'You never get paid when you write,' I reminded myself, 'unless you count that time you wrote limericks about irritable bowels for a drug company. You get paid after you write, if it's any good. And it won't be any good if you don't do the research.'

'But this is so hard! I don't know what I'm doing!'

'Whine, whine.'

By this time I was at the library door, unresolved but moving forward. Which is to say alive. A research lesson was in progress, so the parent volunteer, a tall woman with a thick

95

graying braid down her back, showed me to the local history shelves. I took what I could find relating to schools and sat at a dark oak table near the back windows. First I scanned indexes, then I paged through yearbooks, and finally I revisited a *History of Bath* I'd looked at in the Davenport Library the day before. Maybe I'd missed something. The early photos of Pulteney Park interested me, but I didn't find any new information. The yearbooks were a washout, too. After about an hour, I autographed my book for the library, laid it on the circulation desk, and went back downstairs. As I signed out in the office, the jingling secretary asked, "Did you see the ghost?"

"Ghost?" I echoed, my heart speeding up, my afternoon weariness evaporating.

"Oh yes," she said, looking up from her computer. "One of our history teachers used to swear we had a ghost."

"What kind of . . . I mean, anyone in particular?"

"I don't know," the secretary said. "But he sure got the kids' attention!"

"I guess so. Could I talk to him?"

"He's retired," she said. "And probably a snowbird. Winters up here are hard on older folks."

I persisted. "Could I have his name anyway?"

"Sure," she said, and wrote it, along with a phone number from her Rolodex, on a memo square which boasted the words, "If you can read this, thank a teacher" around an apple logo.

"Thanks," I said, and walked out into waning light. For good measure, I said Thanks to Jane too. Gray clouds rumpled the horizon like a comforter at the foot of the bed. I looked at my watch: 2:30 and I hadn't had lunch. I'd drive through McDonald's and check in at the Day's Inn. Fast food lunch on top of bacon and egg breakfast: sheesh. Even my pen would clog up at this rate!

CZ

The first thing I did at my Days Inn desk was try the number the secretary had given me. As the phone rang and rang, I peeled the tops back from the plastic half-and-half containers and whitened my coffee, remembering how as a little girl I'd loved those miniature milk bottles that sat on the saucer of each cup of coffee grown-ups got in a restaurant. Clear glass and tall as a child's thumb, they had a thick cardboard lid crimped snug around the top. My parents took cream in their coffee, but my daddy's mama didn't, so when Jo was with us, she passed the little bottles to me and I made a ritual of prying off the paper disk and drinking the sweet cream.

I felt a stab of longing for this grandmother, who had died just a year before my father. Why was I looking at strangers' graves when I had my kin to mourn for? Just then the retired teacher's answering machine came on. I left my question, along with contact information and hung up. Maybe even if he was in Florida, he would check his messages. (In fact, I never heard from him.)

Promising myself I would visit those graves in Resthaven soon, I unwrapped my grilled chicken sandwich. Despite its crepe-paper lettuce and wheel of pink, hard tomato, it made my mouth water. With a little salt and pepper, it would be tasty. But after I took a bite, I realized I was hungry for something else too. Words. Ink. A flow of reflection, some-place to put the feelings of this day. I reached in my briefcase for a yellow legal pad, then dug out my favorite pen of the time, a brown Pilot Razorpoint. I closed my eyes, waiting for what might come. I began speaking to Jane.

That graveyard I wandered in, were you not there, too, looking for me? Those stones, those deep names, are they doors?

I come to where you called me. I come back. And you -- where are you? In the golden grass of a field where your house stood? In the thumbprint whorl at the bottom of the holy water font?

There's a fieldstone marker to the left of your par-ents' graves. Gray-streaked and coppery, jagged. And I feel as I see it that the stone fits some place inside me, that I have an emptiness just that shape.

This must be the grave of the real Jane Grace.

I am a stranger here, in this cemetery, on this road. The dead are strangers to me. I am searching where I know nothing for what I can't explain. I am gone into Beyond.

And in Beyond, these are my people, living and dead. All the stones are the ones I'm looking for. "Gone, ye blessed . . .," the inscription reads, and I feel the chisel cut into my stone heart. "Our Boy," and I see him run, a two-year-old still in dresses, down the wide poplar boards of the front hall. "Our best/ we gave/ to the angels."

I stood up after I wrote this. Looking out the window at the anonymous strip of gas stations and fast food huts, I felt a little shaky. Who knew where I was? Who knew when?

Oh, don't be ridiculous, I told myself. You're a writer in a motel. Now write! I bent over, hands to the floor, to stretch

98

out my shoulders, then got back to work. I expected the second Jane to speak now, Jane who was Ruth. But sitting in a chair lined with motel pillows to make me tall enough for the desk, breathing the acrid air of a room just declared *No Smoking*, what I wrote was this:

Don't come looking for me to tell you nothing. Here I lie, just fine, praise Him, and my bones is still and unburdened. My Spirit – Justified! Sanctified! – is off with the hallelujah angels, and you wanting to talk with these bones. To know their story. Huh! Hear about their skinny portion in life.

Want me to tell about the Rev. Robert Campbell, who owned me, and give me to his daughter, Lucy, when we was four. That was up at Saratoga, before he hauled us out here. He owned my brother Jehu too. Said he would free us just as soon as he could afford it. And Jehu said – to me, not to the Reverend's long, mournful face – "But Rev. Mr. Robert Campbell, sir, we cannot afford to be slaves."

Wish you could hunt up Jehu's bones and talk to him. He had a mind strong as his back. Jehu would have got us to Canada for sure, if the river hadn't took him.

Of course, I lived on after Emancipation, long past the laying out of that lanky white man, but the truth is, when the jubilation bell finally rung, I was too old to be free. Lucy – Teeple she was then, married to George, sober-faced as her pa – Lucy and I was like two trees growed together. Wasn't it me who eased her babies in? Helped lay her dead folks out? And pulled teeth, cured warts, and got her runt, Solomon, through the Summer Complaint.

Lucy kept me from jumping in the river that fall I pure lost my mind over Jehu. And when I went blind, she helped me learn to run that old house in the dark.

Yes, my bones is here, you don't need to go dows-

ing. Here, just like Lucy's, just as white. But listen: My old life you come looking for, and yours about half used-up you drug along, tribulation that they be, they pass off like a bad dream. They ain't nothing to what comes after. Just God clearing His throat, fixing to sing.

20

The next morning I'd arranged to have breakfast with Emma Jones before starting the long drive back across New York. We met at a homestyle restaurant just outside of town. To my surprise, this small energetic gray-haired be-speckled woman brought her husband and grown daughter with her. The four of us slid into a green leatherette booth as if we were family.

Emma explained that Deborah, her daughter, had just lost her husband to cancer the week before and needed to get out of the house. This threw me. I didn't know these people. In the presence of such grief, how were we going to come up with an hour or so's worth of conversation? We couldn't talk about past lives and ghosts.

"I'm so sorry," I said to Deborah, whose eyes were red-rimmed, whose hands trembled. She smoothed her dark hair, already clasped tight at the nape of her neck.

"Oh, I know Ernie's all right," she said. "His suffering's over. It's me and the kids I'm worried about."

I was going to respond to this when the waitress came

and we ordered from our plastic, syrup-spotted menus. She poured coffee, fresh and stout, as my grandmother used to say.

"I told them about your search," Emma said after the waitress moved on.

I swallowed in surprise. Coffee burned the back of my throat. "You did?"

"Sure," she said. "Isn't that okay?"

I looked at them: Emma and Ray her husband, solid in their sixties, RV travelers; Deborah, their grief-shocked daughter. They'd come out to eat with me in the midst of their loss. I let out the breath I didn't know I'd been holding. "It's okay," I said.

"I'm a dowser," Ray announced.

Another surprise. "You find water?" I asked lamely. I'd never met a dowser before.

"Not Ray," Emma said with a laugh, resting her hand on his arm.

"He finds graves," Deborah put in.

"Graves?" Were we going to talk about graves when they'd just buried Ernie?

"That's right," Ray said. "Sometimes there's no marker. But all you need to tell where a body lies is patience and a coat hanger."

"And a gift," Emma added.

"Some say that," Ray conceded. "I think anyone willing to try could probably do it."

"It's the willingness then," I ventured.

"You bet," he said, his blue eyes sparkling.

I felt a rush of kinship with this man. "Writing's like

102

that, too," I told them.

The waitress arrived with her many-plated tray and began dealing out eggs (fried and scrambled), French toast, waffles, English muffins.

"I'll grab your juice and some fresh coffee and be right back," she promised.

Emma, Ray, and I all sampled the food she'd set before us and started passing the salt, pepper, Country Spread, and syrup. Deborah just looked at her plate.

"You've got to eat, Deb," her mother told her.

She nodded, then looked at me, seated next to her like sister or cousin or friend. "For the kids," she said, her eyes filling with tears. She buttered her waffles, drizzled on the syrup, then using her fork, cut away a bite which she put into her mouth. It looked good but she made a face.

"I didn't think you liked sweet things for breakfast," Emma said.

Deborah swallowed. "I don't," she said.

My guess was that Ernie liked waffles, but I didn't say anything. The juice arrived, three oranges and one tomato. And more coffee.

"So have you found anything on your visit?" Emma asked.

"Not a lot," I told her. "I did visit the Teeple graves. They're in Hope Cemetery."

"You got my letter then?" she asked, spreading grape jelly on her toast.

"No. What letter?"

She raised her eyebrows above her glasses. "I sent it last week so you'd know to go there when you came. I'd just located the family in the cemetery records."

I laughed. "I didn't get the letter," I said, "but I did get the idea. It just seemed that if they'd lived at Campbell, they'd likely be buried there." Truth to tell, I was glad I hadn't gotten the letter; it felt good to have found this on my own. It was reassuring as I thought about going to Wales.

"So you saw Ruth's grave, too?"

"What?"

"No, of course not. You didn't know she'd married."

"Married? My Ruth?" I felt like someone had struck my chest with a hammer.

"That's right," Emma went on, as if we were talking over the back fence and this was good news. "That's why she disappears from the census. She married a doctor, Leander Sutherland, and moved to Galesburg, Illinois. In 1874, I think. It's in the letter."

Eggs and toast were tumbling in my stomach like wash. I couldn't get out any words.

But I didn't need to. Emma went on, "She came back here toward the end of her life and lived with her niece. It's in the obituary I found."

"Thanks," I said, pushing the word past the knot in my throat, reaching for other words to anchor the free fall I was in. Galesburg. Wales. Carl Sandburg. Dylan Thomas. Hogbutchers. Poets. Swansea. Landlocked. All those swans I drew as a kid. Ruth. Jane. What was I supposed to do?

I came back to the moment in time to hear Emma say, "If there was an announcement of that wedding, I haven't found it yet. But I'll keep looking."

"Good," I said, and swallowed. There were eggs on my

tongue. I'd been sitting there, just stopped, with egg on my tongue.

"That's the best I can do," Deborah said, pushing her plate away. She'd eaten a quarter of the two waffles and half a piece of bacon. We're watching her like you watch a kid, I thought. How can I feel bereft in the face of such loss?

"It's a start," Ray said. "There'll be lunch later."

The waitress came with the check, which I picked up.

"Hold on –," Ray protested.

"No, please. Emma won't let me pay her. This is my treat."

He hesitated.

"I can take it off on taxes," I told him.

"All right," he said.

In no time the waitress had returned with credit card and receipts. I signed and we were on our way.

Our way split at the parking lot, of course. I wasn't part of this wounded family, though I'd felt included as we ate together. Or maybe I was connected to them, just as I'd glimpsed stories of other griefs in the cemetery. "Our best/ we gave/ to the angels."

Standing between cars, we all hugged goodbye, our words turning to clouds in the chill air.

"I'll have you in my prayers," I said to Deborah, who felt thin beneath her down coat.

"My kids, too," she said. "Kevin, Kim, and Lily."

"Of course," I promised. "Thanks again, Emma. Good to meet you, Ray." And then I was pulling out on the road bound for New York City. Confused, hurt, humbled. A little oddly elated. And Ruth-less.

21

It's a good thing I didn't have a cell phone that day. I would have used up a month of minutes calling Steve, calling Ann, reaching out to friends in my writers group to talk me across the shock and the miles. She married? She moved to Illinois? Was this some kind of joke?

It was one thing to discover that Jane Grace wasn't really her name. The proximity of Ruth the schoolteacher in the same family and her eventual disappearance suggested an explanation for that. Her taking Jane's name had come to feel like fact to me. I no longer troubled over it.

But this? Didn't this sweep away the whole story the way a flood carries off a riverbank house? And I'd applied for those grants. Good Lord! What if I got one? Could I say: *"Oh, I beg your pardon. Did I say I wanted to go to Wales? I meant Galesburg. They do sound alike."* I didn't think so. Could I just say, "Thanks, but no thanks. I made a mistake"? There'd be plenty of writers and artists on the waiting list, praying for a little money for ink or paint and rent.

Be realistic, I told myself as I sped through tawny and

platinum fields. The grants, which you probably won't get anyway, are the least of your problems. What about all this work? What about all you knew as a child that drew you back to Bath? The floodgate of tears that opened in St. Mary's? All the facts from past-life sessions that *do* match the records?

My head was starting to hurt and I had at least two hours' more driving. The last part would be the challenge: Friday afternoon traffic north of New York City, returning the Mirage to the White Plains airport, getting a cab to the hotel in time. Going over this only made me more tense and I resolved to stop in a bit, get some crackers and fruit for lunch – no more grease! – and try to think about something else.

I started singing. Unbidden, the song that came to me was "Gotta Get Along Without You Now." This struck me as so apt, I started to laugh. I'd been jilted! So I tried to come up with other songs appropriate to my situation. The next one was "I'll Be Seeing You."

Halfway through the verse, I stopped. That wouldn't do! It made me think of my father, who'd loved a recording of Mario Lanza singing it, and that brought tears. Was this whole thing really a search for Daddy? A wild attempt to 'prove' to myself that he wasn't really gone? To recreate a childhood trip when he was young and strong and I sat in the back seat singing "Hey There"?

As I pondered this, a sentence, like a sign in the road, appeared in my head:

"I married for my mother's sake."

I stopped singing. I most certainly did *not* marry for

107

my mother's sake. Both my parents were supportive but uncertain about my choice. And Steve's parents didn't want him to marry at all –

"To spare her the scandal."

But there wasn't – we weren't – oh. Oh, not me. Ruth. The baby. "You did what?" I asked out loud over the steering wheel.

No inner voice spoke back.

"Come on!" I said angrily. "If you're going to talk to me, talk!"

She didn't.

"This is not fair!" I said, my voice rising. "Why don't you tell the truth?"

I wasn't crying now. I was mad. And driving too fast. Not good. At the next likely-looking exit I got off and hunted some lunch. When I merged back onto the road, I turned on the radio. Time to pull myself together here. I had to meet my editor that night, give a speech the next day. The past, whatever it was, would have to wait.

22

When I returned from New York, there were more jobs and Christmas preparations – the extended family was coming to our house – extra choir rehearsals and church services, and then Christmas itself. After that, we went to my mother's for New Year's, so it wasn't until the dawn of 1999 that I got back to Jane Grace.

Or whoever. I was dispirited about the whole project. Any direction I might start out in would just double back to this ridiculous place where I found myself now. What was the point? Was my work making fun of me?

So when the letter from the Kentucky Arts Council came saying that I didn't get their fellowship, I was almost relieved. That was one plate of crow I wouldn't have to eat. However, soon after that missive hit the bottom of our red letter box, it was followed by one from the Kentucky Foundation for Women awarding me $1000. That was less than I had asked for, but enough to pay for my plane ticket and some lodging, more or less, depending on the current fares and exchange rate. My heart lifted in spite of myself, in spite of my nagging head which knew what it knew.

'She didn't go to Wales, you idiot! It would be absurd for you to take this money and make this trip when you know she was in Galesburg.'

But did I know? The only documentation I had was the obituary, which until that moment I hadn't thought to question. Okay, I said to myself, let me make sure that she really was a Galesburg matron and I'll give this up. Enough is enough.

I called the Galesburg Historical Society and spoke to a message machine. No one returned my call, so after a few days I tried the public library. Yes, they had a local history volunteer, but she was only in on Wednesdays. Sometimes she could help people over the phone. It depended. Winter was busy for genealogists. With gardens frozen, folks had more time to dig for family roots.

The next week I reached Lib Yoder, the volunteer. "Sutherland?" she echoed when I told her who I was looking for. "That doesn't ring a bell."

"I know you have tons of queries," I ventured, "but if there's any way you can look into this soon, I'd appreciate it. I've got a grant —"

"Everybody's in a hurry," she said, cutting off my explanation. "You'd think these ancestors were kids lost in the mall, considering how hyper people get."

I laughed.

"But I'll do what I can. Let me read you back your information...."

While I was waiting to hear from her, I checked the fare to London. It had gone down $300 since I'd made my budget for the grant! I penciled in a time to go: the last two weeks in February, before Lent complicated Steve's church schedule and before the spring fare hike.

I also discovered there had been razor blade factories in the Bath area at one time. One was south of Steuben County; two were north. So either version of the family story would work. We could have come upon it whether we went to Niagara Falls or not.

Even as I checked the airfare, I was still mad at Jane/Ruth or whoever was leading me on this not-so-merry chase. I felt as if I had acted in good faith while she was behaving like Coyote in the trickster tales: hiding, shape-shifting, causing my tenuous hold on her story to fall apart. I tried to write in her voice but nothing came. As we say in the mountains, she had sulled up. Or maybe she knew I was really in no mood to listen.

Then I came in one evening after two days' work in Cincinnati schools to find this message on the answering machine:

Mrs. Lyon, this is Lib Yoder at the Galesburg Public Library. I'm afraid I can't find a trace of Ruth or Leander Sutherland. If he was a doctor here, he should appear in the city directory for that time, but he doesn't. He's not in the census either. I hate to say this, but unless the dates you gave me are wrong, I'm afraid we've hit a dead end.

"Yes!" I said, pumping my fists in the air and dancing around the answering machine.

111

Steve heard me and came down the hall. "What is it?" he asked.

"Houston," I said grinning, "we are go for Wales."

23

The next afternoon, after I'd bought my ticket, Steve and I went to an Irish pub downtown to raise a pint.

"To Wales!" he said lifting his Guinness.

"To Jane Grace!" I added clinking with my mug of ale.

My elation from the day before had dimmed just a bit. I had to admit that while relieved to discover Ruth couldn't be found in Galesburg, I still had no idea what to do with the fact of her marriage.

"Give yourself time," Steve said. "You've only had this information for a month."

Indeed. It was a month to the day since I had spent that cold morning reading tombstones at Hope Cemetery.

"Besides," Steve went on, "it's only recently that we've had history to confuse us about story."

"What?" My skin prickled. "Say that again."

The waiter showed up with a plate of hot cheesy bacon-sprinkled potato skins. The small thick plates he gave us made a satisfying *chink!* on the wooden table.

"It's only recently," Steve repeated, prying a potato skin

away from its fellows and twirling the cheese string on his finger to break it, "that we've had history to confuse us about story."

There was something thrilling about hearing him say that, about being released into a larger view.

Truly, I married him for his ability to think like this. (Okay, there was also his music and humor and blue-black hair.)

"Say more," I requested.

"We worship facts now the way we used to worship story," he went on. "They're our standard for truth. Other ways – spirit ways – of knowing we mistrust and discredit."

"So you're saying that Ruth's marrying Leander doesn't mean she never went to Wales?"

"Yes, but more than that. I'm saying that in the realm of your experiencing Jane Grace, dates and facts may not matter all that much."

I could feel the ale taking effect. All of a sudden my thoughts were above my head and I had to pull them down like balloons. I ate a potato skin for ballast. When was I going to commit to healthy food?

Steve let the silence be. Another winning quality.

"So you're saying that if I don't find her in Wales, it doesn't mean she didn't go?"

"I'm saying that we don't know what her world is like. Maybe in this universe, the one that has the census books where you found her in Bath, she did marry this doctor and do whatever –"

"Then why doesn't she –"

"Hold on. But in a parallel universe she got pregnant

114

and went to Wales."

"I can't deal with that!" I said, suddenly exasperated. "If I start thinking about parallel universes, how can I know anything?"

"Maybe you're experiencing one," Steve said.

Brilliant a minute ago, he seemed smug and irritating now. Oh, I should never drink beer in the afternoon . . . .

"You have to trust that something real is going on," he continued, "even if you can't explain it."

"Why?" I challenged.

"Because that's all you've got," he said simply.

The waiter swung by and Steve ordered another Guinness.

"Story, you mean?"

"Your experience of it at different points," he said. "When you were five, when you returned to Bath, in the past-life sessions, and in the records that do match."

"And in what I'm writing," I offered, starting to feel hopeful.

He nodded.

"So story is larger than history?"

Steve took a drink from his new pint. My ale was gone so he offered me a sip of stout. Ugh! I forget how bitter and disgusting it is, like day-old coffee mixed with water you'd boiled oily car parts in.

"Not just larger but of a different order," Steve insisted. "You know what Jung says."

"I know some of what Jung says," I told him and laughed, remembering how early in our marriage, before children even, Steve had spent months reading through the

Collected Works. It seemed as if everything I said then elicited a quotation from Jung, and eventually Steve wrote the master into the chorus of a country song:

> *We've been washed out by hand*
> *In the blood of the Lamb*
> *And hung out to dry*
> *On the Jungian cross.*

Steve went on, "Jung said, 'Myth is the story that never happened but is always true.'"

"Wait a minute!" I protested. "First you say this could have happened in another reality, that there could be two sets of facts. And now you're saying it may not have happened at all!"

"No, I'm not," he said, calmly bisecting the last potato skin which I declined. "I'm saying that dates and places don't have to line up for your story to be true."

"So I shouldn't be going to Wales at all?" I was stuck on the practical. Easy for him to say the facts didn't matter. He wasn't about to traipse across the ocean in search of them.

"I don't mean that," he assured me. "I just mean you can trust yourself and look for other things as well."

"Like what?"

"Like whatever comes to you," he said.

What came to us was the bill, which I payed with my business credit card. "A meeting for research consultation" I would call it.

Never mind that the consultation – or was it the ale? – was as confusing as it was clarifying. I had Steve's support and that was a big thing. He didn't think my journey deluded or self-indulgent. I would hold onto that, as I did to his arm as we walked back to the car.

24

Then we all got the flu, in staggered and staggering fashion. Not the two-day, throw-up-and-loosen-up variety, but the week-long cough-all-night-and-whimper-in-the-daylight kind. Steve was stricken first and half-way through his misery, Joey's started, and just when I thought I might escape, it hit me. I was supposed to go speak to students in the Vermont College MFA program that week. And when the job was over, I was scheduled to take a bus to Boston for my nephew's graduation as a paramedic.

I hated to miss the graduation and I hate to miss jobs. Vermont's was a low-residency program, meaning students were only there twelve days twice a year, so I couldn't reschedule. I went back and forth about it. Surely I'd feel human in three more days, in two . . . . Finally the program secretary told me to forget it – they'd put me down for summer. Relieved, I switched my worry to what if Steve and Joey got this sick while I was gone? What if I did? Who would take care of us? No mother should go larking off like this. It's unnatural, I thought.

Thank God I knew other mother-writers who also traveled when their work demanded. I remembered a paragraph my friend Louise Borden sent me from her journal about this struggle:

> *The choices for writing . . . begin before which word will follow which word . . . begin earlier . . . choosing to go in the direction of the call . . . choosing to go alone . . . to expose oneself to the loneliness.*

That's just how it is, I told myself. The conflict comes with the territory. No growing without risk. Besides, we've all got flu-immunity now.

So once I was stronger I continued my preparations. From a B & B directory I chose a home base at Pennard Cliffs on the Gower peninsula south of Swansea. I wanted to stay there because Jane had described her joy in wandering the cliffs and painting the sea. Then there was the question of transportation inside Wales. Did I want to rent a car for the freedom it would give me or travel by train and take more restricted routes? I decided on the latter because I'd heard wild tales from my brother about driving on the wrong side of twisty English roads which seemed barely one and a half lanes wide. I wouldn't see anything with my eyes clamped to the road. And in winter driving conditions would be worse. Through AAA I ordered a BritRail pass. And where exactly was I going to travel?

In my *Pallas Wales* guidebook I found a photo of the Inigo Jones Bridge from the beach puzzle. It was in Llanrwst, a village a little south of Conwy which is on the Irish Sea. I definitely wanted to see that, along with the coal country towns of Merthyr Tidfal, Afan, and Aberfan. Jane had mentioned a town that sounded like Afan or Athan and these were the closest names I could locate.

Finally I packed. Even without the flu, I went hot and cold as I filled the suitcase. But I was committed. Wild goose or no, it was my chase. And I'd only be gone twelve days – not a drastic absence.

As I prepared my belongings, I tried to prepare myself. I might find nothing. It won't be a failure, I told myself. Trust the process. Whatever you find will be what you went for. At the very least you'll come back knowing what the country looks and feels like. It will be easier to imagine Jane there.

Now it happened that my brother Robert, who is an English professor, had taken students to London that semester. He and his wife Betty were living in the university's flat near Muswell Hill and they invited me to spend my first night with them, visiting and recovering from jet lag. I liked that idea. It would be anchoring.

However, a day or so before I was to depart, Robert called. "I'm so disappointed," he began, "but I'm going to miss you. My colleague revised the schedule and we're taking the students to Bath that day. It's an overnight too."

Bath? I couldn't believe it. Jane had written for her brother to be in Bath on the day she left –

"But Betty would love to see you. If you'll still stop over, she'll skip the Bath jaunt. We've both been there anyway."

"Oh, sure," I said hardly able to stay in the conversation. He doesn't know the story, I reminded myself. He can't see how wild this is, this pattern reasserting itself.

"Georgie," – that's what my family calls me – "are you there?"

"Oh, yes, sorry. So what should I do?"

"Just take the train from Gatwick as we planned and Betty will meet you at Victoria Station."

"Where?" I asked.

"As you come in from the train if she's on time. Otherwise wait at the big W.H. Smith bookstore in the center."

"Okay," I said.

"I really hate to miss you. Any chance you could stay with us as you leave, too?"

"I'll think on it," I told him. "I'm sorry to miss you too."

All I could do when I hung up was laugh. This is so bizarre, I thought – like Jane's story is waving at mine. It must mean I'm on the right track.

25

After an easy flight and a hard-working sojourn with Betty – she helped me proof the galleys of a poetry-writing handbook I then FedExed to the publisher in Texas – I caught the train at Paddington Station for Wales. I'd hoped to make the 11 a.m. departure, but due to a computer glitch at Leicester Square it left just as I arrived. Betty and I dragged my luggage, along with sandwiches from The Upper Crust, to a bench on the main concourse and had an early lunch.

"So what are you going to do when you get to Swansea?" she asked.

I held up my hand for more chewing time on the baguette, then said "Search records, visit towns where I think she might have been, wander on the coast . . . "

"You couldn't pay me to do that sort of thing," Betty declared. "Not by myself."

"Oh, I won't be alone," I joked. "I'll have a ghost with me."

"Very funny."

We finished our crunchy, sharp-sweet ham-and-swiss

sandwiches in silence. I gave Betty the phone number for the B and B before boarding and promised to call about stopping over on my return.

On this winter Sunday afternoon, second class on the Great Western was packed. As we pulled out I watched an elderly lady at the window opposite read Italian vocabulary. Then a little boy in orange and blue toddled into me as he and his mother made their way to the W.C. Once we cleared the train shed, we were blessed with sun pouring through the windows, glittering grime on tracks and platforms, then stippled by moving clouds as we picked up speed and made our rocking way west.

CR

It was dark when the train pulled into Swansea – a gray-blue misty shawl of dark. I hadn't reckoned on that. I don't know why. It was winter, I should have known. But I forget how far north the British Isles are and how the sea weaves in its own evening.

Walking into the station lobby I paused to touch the painted crest of Swansea on the wall. Beneath my all-weather coat and turtleneck sweater my heart felt full of joy and trepidation. I was really here. Whatever happened or didn't, I had come this far. I had kept that *vow* printed large and blue over Jane's voice and mine. I had crossed the *deep blue sea*.

26

I hailed a cab in the circle in front of Swansea Station and was soon speeding on my way to Heatherlands Bed and Breakfast. The mist was so thick I could make out only lights from cars and nearby buildings. My first glimpse of Dylan Thomas' "ugly, lovely town" would have to wait till morning.

The young, curly-headed cabbie didn't talk, which was fine with me. I was as tired and hungry as I was excited, and since I couldn't see Oystermouth Bay or Kittle or the Beaufort Arms or anything else we were passing, I dozed for the twenty minutes or so the ride took. When the little cab jerked to a halt and the cabbie said, "£18, Miss," I climbed out into fog and dug for a £20 note by porch light while he set my luggage on the cobbled drive. Before I could realize I'd been gouged, he was gone. I shouldered my briefcase, then wheeled my suitcase to the door and wrestled myself into a small parlor where a white-haired woman in a lavender sweater sat behind a reception desk. She looked up at me quizzically.

"I have a reservation," I began.

She gave a dry laugh that ended in a little cough.

"You're a bit early aren't you, dearie?"

Early? But it's dark, I thought. And anyway I didn't give them an arrival time.

"Isn't this Heatherlands Bed and Breakfast?" I asked.

The woman laughed again, this time rocking her head back and forth. I looked around the parlor then. Somehow it didn't look like a B and B. It looked like people lived here. And there was a walker folded by the door.

"No, love. I'm afraid you've come to the wrong place. This is Heatherslade Rest Home. Heatherlands is just a ways down the road."

"But I don't have a car," I said. "I took a cab."

"Never you mind. I'll just ring up Bertie."

Bertie?

After a quick, cheery phone call, she said, "Bertie will pop round and pick you up."

"Thank you."

Another cough. "And where do you come from?" she asked, patting her breast as you would a baby.

"Kentucky."

"Play the horses, do you?"

"Not really," I said.

"Good girl," she told me, as if I were ten. "I'm afraid I'd lose my pension."

I could picture this laughing, coughing, lavender old woman standing by the paddock at Keeneland . . .

A motor purred close outside, a car door slammed, and tall, ruddy-faced Bertie Churchill appeared in the door.

"You must be Mrs. Lyon," he said, holding out his hand.

"Yes," I said, grateful to be recognized, glad for his warm touch.

"Sorry for the confusion," he said. "Deadhead cabbies!"

"I'm sorry you had to come get me," I replied.

"No trouble," he said, opening the door, then picking up my bag and briefcase as easily as if they were empty.

"Thank you, Evelyn," he called as he nodded his head for me to go first.

"Yes, thanks," I echoed, looking back at her.

"Not at all," she said, with a sparkle in her voice. "I'll have something to tell the girls in the morning."

Outside I stood while Bertie put my bags in the boot of a car even smaller than the cab. Then he came around and opened the door for me.

"I hope your trip was pleasant," he said backing out into the mist.

"Very much so," I told him. "I only came from London today."

"My wife tells me you're here to do research," he said, speeding down a tiny road through a wall of fog.

Or get killed, I thought. "Yes. I'm a writer."

"Well, you've come to a place rich in history."

"I'm eager to see it," I said, then laughed a shallow ha-ha.

Bertie gave a musical chuckle. He was beautiful, I realized all at once, his white hair and sharp nose, his big hands. "I'm afraid it's like this from about four o'clock on in winter," he said, making a sharp turn left and then left again into his driveway. "Here we are," he said, and sprang out his door, then dashed around to open mine.

As I got out, a slender gray-haired woman opened the white door of the cottage. "Go meet Gwyn," he said, "I'll fetch your bags."

After a gracious welcome, Gwyn showed me down the hall to a pink and white bedroom complete with a tiny TV, a tea table with electric kettle beside a basket of tea and biscuits, and a vanity which would serve as a desk. My stomach growled. "It's lovely," I said, and indeed everything was meticulously clean and comfortable. Bertie brought in my belongings, then backed out of the small room.

"The w.c. is across the hall," Gwyn said. "You're our only guest at the moment so you'll have it all to yourself."

"Thanks."

"All settled then?" she asked. And before I could answer, went on, "What time will you be wanting breakfast?"

"First I need to get supper," I blurted. "Is there a restaurant nearby I could walk to?"

"Not at this hour," she said. "You wash up and Bertie will drive you round to the pub."

"I hate to cause him more trouble," I said.

"Don't think of it. He loves to get out."

So that's how I wound up chauffeured to the Gower Inn, situated on an invisible golf course, eating plaice and chips, drinking a half pint of bitter, at who knows what hour in a fog-wrapped, half-timbered, arcade-game-lit pub. I couldn't help thinking how I came looking for a ghost and the cabbie took me to the home of ghosts-in-waiting. Heatherlands/Heatherslade: just a syllable's difference. Another turn of phrase and you're thin air.

127

27

By eight the next morning I was seated alone at one end of a lace-covered table that could have served eight. Long windows to my right revealed a beautiful asymmetrical garden, enclosed by hedge and graced by small trees in the far corners, bare now, poised like dancers.

"How can you have a garden so lovely in February?" I asked Gwyn as she poured coffee and set a crystal glass of orange juice down by my plate.

"It's the mist," she told me. "The sea winds keep us from getting too cold. And Bertie is out there every chance he gets pottering about."

"In winter?" I asked.

She laughed. "He's one of those men who has to swim naked in the sea year round. He says it strengthens his blood."

The breakfast she put before me a few minutes later was a feast: grilled tomatoes and mushrooms, fried eggs, fat sausages, and baked beans along with a rack of toast. It looked and smelled wonderful, but it seemed only moments before that I'd eaten all that fish and chips. I vowed to have a snack for lunch and an early supper in order to do justice to Gwyn's cooking . . .

As I munched, I studied the Swansea Transit timetable and other brochures I'd found in the room. Those sausages – oh my, too much of something. Oatmeal? I couldn't tell, but they were a little frightening. The mushrooms were delicious, however. Just a plate of mushrooms and toast would do me fine.

Thirty minutes later I stepped out of Heatherlands to make my short trek to the bus stop. It was sunny now, the grass Easter green, the stones of walls and houses glittering with the wet.

Turning right at the end of the Churchill's street I almost bumped into three shaggy ponies grazing on the berm in front of the house. Dark brown, golden, and tawny, they paid me no mind as I marveled past them. Later I learned they were part of a herd of wild ponies which has the run of the Gower. They have owners, who keep them shod and see to their health, but they don't have fences. The sky is their barn roof and their hoofprints are everywhere.

CR

Perversely, I didn't do at all what I'd planned that day. When the bus let me off at the Quadrant Centre – a bus station with mall attached, a mall which boasts Tennessee Ice Cream – I studied my map and struck out north on Castle Street, then west on Mansel Street and Walter Road till I came to the Uplands, the section of Swansea Dylan Thomas called home.

I climbed Cymdonkin Drive, which my grandmother would have called "steep as a cow's face," to stand in front of number 5, where he spent his childhood. Because I'd practically worn out my Caedmon record of Thomas reading "Fern Hill" and "Do Not Go Gentle," and *A Child's Christmas in Wales*, I could hear his voice as I stood there, its bell and bellow and benediction. Was this really the loom his voice was woven on, this gray-brown, stone-fenced street punctuated by a green dumpster labeled CELTIC WASTE?

I made my way to the neighborhood park, threading the curved path around the pond till I came to his monument, a granite boulder smooth-dressed on one side to make a tablet for his words:

> *Time held me green and dying*
> *Though I sang in my chains like the sea.*

In college I had painted those words on poster board in pearly blue above wild green waves and taped them to my bedroom wall. Now here I stood, in the thick middle of my life, a startled pilgrim. This wasn't where I was going, was it? This wasn't why I had come.

Touched, cold, and over-upholstered I made my way back down to Walter Street and over to the city center where I stopped in a tea shop to regulate my temperature and gather my wits.

What was wrong with me? I hadn't come all this way to be a literary sightseer. I had so little time – what was I thinking? I swore as I sipped my tea and ate Welsh cakes – buttery, pastry cookie confections – that as soon as I finished I would ask directions to the Records Office and get myself back on track.

I didn't though. Once out the door I headed toward the River Tawe, Somerset Place, and the Dylan Thomas Centre.

Truth to tell, I'm still a little embarrassed by this. I spent my entire and only Monday in Wales avoiding what I'd come to do! Oh, I can say I was grounding myself in my earlier ties to Swansea, in my teenage poet days "young and easy under the apple boughs." I was affirming and consolidating who I was in this life and what had drawn me to this place. But I was also postponing the search I had come for. Brave enough to follow Jane's hide-and-seek story across the ocean, still I was afraid. What if after all this I didn't find her? What if I did?

28

The next day I set off for the Guildhall, which my guidebook listed as the Records Office. It was quite a hike and, much to my dismay, turned out to be the repository for municipal records when what I needed were county records. So, with overstuffed briefcase and false economy, I turned around and cold-footed it to the other location. Why didn't I take a cab? Not in budget, having been gouged by the first cab driver. Not in vocabulary. This is one of the perils of traveling alone: you are limited to your own mind, which may shrink in new surroundings. A companion would have said, "Hey, time is more important here than money!" and I would have agreed and hailed a cab, but as it was I just kept trudging.

It was 10:30 by the time I arrived at the Records Office with its dark satiny tables and deep hush. The receptionist, pencil-thin with long blond hair and heavy black glasses, informed me that I had to fill out a form and pay a fee to use the archives. Once processed, I could request in writing the volumes I needed and they would be brought to me. This would take a while, because of the crowd. Tuesdays were not good days to come, due to their being closed on Mondays.

I was so struck by how this woman echoed the dragon of the public library where I grew up, who made it clear that her job was to guard the books from just such a hooligan as you, that I didn't realize for a minute or two that if I'd stuck to my original plan and come here yesterday I couldn't have gotten in.

After completing the form, I handed it to a clerk, along with £10 and a slip of paper with the following request:

I'm searching for a schoolteacher named Jane Grace. I think she lived in Glamorgan from the 1870's through 1900. I'm also interested in records from the same period in Aberfan.

The clerk, a tall young man trying to grow a golden beard, looked at the paper doubtfully. "*Grace* is not a Welsh name," he said. "To find both that surname and this Christian name – well, it's very unlikely."

"Thanks for the encouragement," I replied, smiling. I liked this fellow with his slate-blue sweater and his starter beard. I could be his mother.

"Oh, I just meant . . . ." He looked down, flustered. "Don't be disappointed, that's all."

"I was joking," I told him. "It's okay."

He gave me a startled look, as if I'd laughed in an operating room. Then he smiled, too. His eyes were navy blue.

"I'll pull some books for you," he said. "Come this way."

I followed him to the one windowless corner of the room, fitted out with slanted tables like oversize dictionary stands. He gestured for me to sit down, then went from shelf to shelf and came back with three big books.

"Here you are," he said, laying them in front of me the way you might place the chalice on an altar.

"Thanks," I said.

As he walked away, I laid my hand on the stack of books where he'd said I wouldn't find her. I prayed to the patron saint of Wild Goose Chases. Then I took a deep breath and opened the first volume. It was bound in amber leather, its corners chipped and bumped. In a celebration of loop and letter-blade the title page read:

Parish Records
County of Glamorgan
1750-1850

Those weren't the years I wanted, so I took up the second one: 1851-1900. Now we were in business.

Excited at first, I turned the large pages and scanned the faded script with rapt attention. But after an hour or so, my eyes and my brain began to tire. I came to the last page. The clerk was right: she wasn't there. Not a single Grace among all those Morgans and Jones.

I couldn't leave without looking through the other books, though. While it didn't make sense to search for her in the earlier years, could I honestly say that sense was what I was making here? Not common sense, that was for sure. I opened the book.

And after about twenty minutes of knotted shoulders and squinted eyes I found:

Jane Grace
b. 1768
Llancarvan, Glamorgan

Yes! There she was! Bleary-eyed, I looked up for someone to share this with, but saw only bent heads beneath green-
shaded reading lamps. I could go tell the clerk – I was half-way
out of my seat to do this – oh, but the date was wrong and my
Jane wasn't born here anyway. It didn't make sense! What
was I supposed to do with this? The right name, which the
clerk told me I wouldn't find, in the right county, but born too
soon, born here, in Wales, over sixty years before Ruth/Jane
was born in New York, maybe thirty years before the birth of
the real Jane Grace.

But wait a minute. Slaves were often given family
names. Could there be a connection between this Jane Grace
and the Teeple family? I'd already established that there were
many Welsh immigrants in that part of New York.

You are grasping at straws, I told myself. No, it's thin-
ner that that: at the shadows of straws.

I went on reading. This Jane married John Phillips in
1790. A child farther down the page may or may not have
been born to them. There was no death date.

Maybe she emigrated, I thought. Maybe that's the
link.

Maybe I'm nuts. I have to be nuts. Now I'm making up
a life for this woman I know nothing about. I'm pushing her
out of this elegant script and across the ocean to balance my
Jane's coming here. My Jane? The Jane who was really Ruth?
Who actually married and then went God knows where.

My head hurt. My heart hurt. I looked around the room again, envying nearby busy patrons – a bald-headed man, a woman in a rose wool dress with steel gray hair, close clipped; a college-age girl with bright red hair clasped at the nape of her neck and splashing down her back. They knew what they were doing, I was sure of it. They had real, absolute ancestors to search for, ghosts who belonged to them, who'd fathered and mothered them, however many generations back. They weren't looking for someone they might have been. Nobody else was searching for a name they had read in a trance.

So what? another side of me countered. You found it, didn't you? Against all odds, here is her name, just as you found it in the Steuben County Records Office. No, it's not her. But that wasn't her either. That was Jane the servant who had been the slave. If you were going for absolute matches, you wouldn't be here. And as for the date, remember what Steve said: it's only recently that we've had history to confuse us about story.

Well, it's working, I thought. I'm certainly confused. I scanned the rest of the book in my hands and found only two other Graces. Three in the whole parish, and one of them was Jane. Something, something was pulling me, some connection I couldn't define.

I took up the third volume, which covered the Rhondda, that area *Pallas Wales* called "the valley of coal and tears." I turned brittle pages till I came to Aberfan. I already planned to go there. Straws. Straws.

Obstinate, I skimmed the lists, page after musty page. And then – my Lord! My eyes came into focus and I caught my breath. There was a whole *list* of Graces! No initial J, but the name the clerk had dismissed as "not Welsh" was flourishing in these Aberfan records. Of all the towns I could have picked, I chose this one because of what Jane had said. I had said. Back in Laura's vivid office. And here they were: Graces abounding.

What it meant, I had no idea, but that it meant, I felt sure. As soon as I copied these names and grabbed some lunch – my stomach was growling despite Gwyn's morning feast – I would locate the Tourist Office and plan my trip to Aberfan. Local records there could tell me more about the Graces. Maybe they would have the key.

29

The train didn't go through Aberfan, so the woman at the Tourist Office suggested I stay at Merthyr Tidfil, a bit north, and double back by bus. For a small fee she booked a B and B for me.

En route the next morning, the train screaked to a stop outside of Cardiff. After five minutes or so, the conductor explained our situation over the loudspeaker. I wrote his words in my journal:

> *Excuse me, ladies and gentlemen. I apologize for the delay but we have a failed train at Cardiff, Queen Street, blocking all service on that line. We'll be stopping at all stations between here and Cardiff Central on the City line. Change here for Llandaff and Cathays.*

That way of working struck me as useful to remember. When a line is closed you keep the trains moving on the other track. You don't declare the trip impossible or quit believing in railroads. You go forward on whatever line remains open. That, I told myself, is exactly what I've been doing.

The trip itself was lovely. In late February the black-faced, black-footed lambs were already in the fields. I saw one ewe with twin lambs standing on either side of her like wings; I saw another lamb try to bound over his mother; too short, he got stuck on her broad, wooly back and she was trying to nose him off. So new, so full of life. The daffodils were out, too, weeks ahead of their appearance at home. St. David's flower and the flower of Swansea, flashing along fence rows as if someone had scattered yellow beads.

Once past Cardiff, I walked down to the buffet car for a cup of coffee. I knew it would be instant and expensive but it would also be hot. A placard on the counter read *Sandwich of the Month: Curried Chicken Mango Wrap.* Just the words delighted me after the endless McBurgers at home.

Once in Merthyr, I stopped in a pub and asked directions to Brynawel B & B. An elderly man put down his pint and walked out onto the sidewalk with me to point the way. "Ta, ta, love!" he called as I walked on, and I almost cried at his kindness. It's being alone like this, I thought, that makes me teary. And then I realized, But I'm not alone. Here is this perfect stranger looking after me.

I got settled in another pink and white room and set out for the tourist office, where I picked up a map and a bus schedule. Buses to Aberfan were frequent and the ride only took thirty minutes, so I slipped into a tiny shop for a lunch of fish and chips. The real thing, served in a cone of newspaper. So nutritionally incorrect. So delicious.

At the bus station an old man got on after me with his cane hung around his neck. Wearing a gray-green-brown coat as old as the world, he looked so wind-worn and so happy that my heart hurt. His bright blue eyes had the same energy as those lambs. What a world, I thought. All you have to do is sit and watch.

But in Aberfan, a just-about-gone town bounded by mountains which themselves looked used up, I had to walk. Town was basically one long street which headed steeply up-hill at the southern end. Half the businesses were closed. In a little newsstand, I asked directions to a records office or a library. The proprietor laughed. "Have to go to Merthyr for books," he said, a cigarette dancing between his lips. "We do have the electric, though."

Back on the street, I found a church, but like all church doors I tried in Wales, it was locked. However, next to it was a bent green sign for the Aberfan Garden of Remembrance. An arrow pointed up that steep hill. Don't you remember? Tombstones would have names, I reckoned, so off I went.

Clouds rolled in as I started up the hill. It was only 2:30 but with the wind picking up, the sky was graying fast. "It's fixing to weather," my grandmother would have said. Oh, good, I thought. I always wanted to be in a graveyard in a for-eign land in a rainstorm.

It didn't feel foreign, though. It gave me a start to real-ize that. Not that I recognized anything – no, it wasn't déjà vu. It was, what? Part of me is at home here, I said to myself. But maybe it's these mountains. Maybe it's these poor people, these coal- and iron-scarred hills.

When the road to the Garden reached what had looked like the top, it made a switchback turn and kept climbing. I imagined horses hauling coffins up this hill, mourners follow-ing on foot behind. I saw trees ahead and an iron gate. Walking through it, I stepped onto earth grown spongy under the inky green of yew trees.

Ready for revelation, I peered at gravestones in the fading light. After a few minutes, I had to laugh, and the sound started blackbirds up from the grass. Most of the inscriptions were in Welsh! I'd never thought of that. It was like a joke, my coming this far in the dimming day to try to read lichenfilled, ice-worn words in a language I didn't even know. Oh, it was this whole absurd trip, really, what was I doing, what did I think I was ever going to find, and who would find me? Here I was, 7,000 miles from home, chasing a ghost . . . .

And then I saw it, a plain, substantial stone. The surname was not Grace, but its chiseled English words caught my heart: *Dead But Still Speaketh.* I felt a current run through my bones. Jane, I said. I am here. Speak to me.

ᚼᚱ

But over the next few days Jane didn't speak. She didn't show up in other records or make her presence felt in walks I took along Pennard Cliffs. The day trip I made to Afan to see the village and the coal mining museum shed no light; if anything, it shed dark. The narrow valley made me homesick for eastern Kentucky, and the cold dismal air chilled me to the bone. Though the guidebook had said "cafe," the museum didn't even offer tea. "Not in winter, you see," the ticket seller told me. So I wandered hungry through dim rooms looking at blurry photos and reading about the number of children who died harnessed to coal carts deep under this earth. It was outrageous.

On the bus back to Swansea, I wrote in my journal:

I had the image today of connecting dots, waiting for the picture to appear. But since the dots aren't numbered, I could crisscross the middle, connect them all, and never get a recognizable outline.

That kind of thinking was no help. What I needed was food. A meat pie. Hot tea. Something to ward off literal and metaphorical cold feet. Back in Swansea I found a little restaurant near the station with a purple handwritten sign in the window proclaiming "Jacket Potatoes!!" Comfort food: just what I needed.

Nobody said this would be easy, I reminded myself ten minutes later, digging into a buttery spud. You knew it wasn't a dot-to-dot affair when you set out. It's not Hollywood either. Nobody's going to step out of the clouds. Your job is to be steady, consistent, down to earth, like this potato.

Yeah, and get cut open and mashed.

Oh, but it was good. And the tea: just right. I felt my blood warm and my fingers and toes start to thaw. My heart lifted too. This is an adventure, I told myself. Just show up, pay attention, and don't judge.

I studied the train schedule. My next goal was to see the puzzle bridge. It would take almost six hours to get there. I'd want to catch the 7:30 out of Swansea. Better head back to Heatherlands then. Better turn in early.

I planned what to pack on the bus ride down the Gower. It was just for one night so I'd use my briefcase as a suitcase. No need to haul the big one with me as I had to Merthyr. And I'd take only one notebook.

I was ready to dispense with this task and get to bed

when I went in the front door, but Gwyn called me from the pass-through to her office.

"You had a call," she said, handing me a slip of paper.

My heart lurched. Oh no. Something was wrong at home . . . Joey . . . my mother . . .

"It's from a lady who does the news in Cardiff. On the telly," she added.

"For me? Why would she call me?"

Gwyn smiled. "I'm a bit curious about that myself," she said.

30

Vivian Morys picked up on the first ring.

"This is George Ella Lyon," I told her. "You wanted to talk to me?"

"Yes, yes! But you're not a man, then?"

"No. Do you need a man?"

She laughed, a glittery sound that made me laugh too. "Not at all," she said. "I just need an American who's been to the Dylan Thomas Centre."

"So that's how you found me – from the register?"

"Precisely. And I'm doing a little feature on Thomas tourism. Could I ask you some questions?"

"Sure."

"Not on the phone," Vivian explained. "On camera."

"You want to put me on – on the telly?" Saying the word tickled me. It was as silly as this situation.

"I do, yes," she said.

"I don't know," I told her. "I'm only here for a few days doing research –"

"You're a scholar, then?" Vivian asked.

"No, a writer –"

"A poet? Like Thomas himself?"

"Yes. I mean, no. I mean, I didn't come here for po-etry. I just love Thomas' work."

"This is so good," Vivian said. "Perfect, really. I can ask you about your work. It won't take long –"

"But I'm taking an early train north tomorrow."

"Going through Cardiff?"

"Yes."

"Give me half an hour at Cardiff Central," she said, full of energy. "Where are you headed?"

"Colwyn Bay and Betws-y-Coed."

"Hold on. Let me check the schedule."

I loved the way she said *shedule*. Did that mean she was English, not Welsh?

"That will work," Vivian said. "If you don't mind being delayed an hour."

Why am I even considering this? I asked myself, even as I moved my lower jaw forward slightly to say yes. This is not what I'm here for. I already spent a day I didn't have on Dylan Thomas. Is it just the glamor of the telly?

"So I'll meet your train," Vivian was saying. "You'll have no trouble spotting me. I'll be the one with the camera."

"I have short brown hair," I told her. "And I'll be wear-ing a navy blue all-weather coat."

"I'll see you at 8:40 then, " she said. "If there's time after the shoot, I'll treat you to tea."

When I hung up I walked back to Gwyn's office where I suspected she'd be waiting to hear what the phone call was about. When I told her, her gray-blue eyes widened and she

145

grew serious. "On the telly? That's quite something. You're an expert then?"

"No," I said. "Just a reader. She wants an American and I happened to turn up."

"You'll be on a Cardiff station – which one, do you know?"

"No, but I'll ask."

"You'll need an early breakfast. What time?"

Gwyn and I settled on mushrooms and toast at 6 a.m. and I packed up and went to bed.

CR

True to her word, Vivian was easy to spot, standing on the platform at Cardiff Central wearing a full-length chocolate brown duster, carrying her tripod over one shoulder and a camera bag slung over the other.

She set up the interview in the large plaza outside the station's main entrance. Young but skillful, Vivian moved us through a quick conversation about my background, my interest in Thomas, and how I happened to be at the museum in Swansea.

Over tea at the station canteen when we finished she said, "You could even quote his poems. That's amazing."

"Not really," I told her. "He's so musical And I started reading him early, when my mind was fresh. Plus I've listened to recordings. His voice inscribed those words on my ear."

My heart, really, I thought, but didn't say it. I felt suddenly shy, sitting at a black-topped table across from this young woman with spiked yellow hair and bright brown eyes.

146

"So tell me about the work that brought you here," she said.

I checked my watch. Seventeen minutes till departure. "It's a long story," I told her. "Would you mind if we take our tea and walk toward the train?"

As we did I gave her a fifty-word version of my quest – I'd boiled it down on the trip from Swansea – and all at once she stopped right under the station's great clock. Dropping her young professional's voice, she said, "I can't believe this!"

"Pardon?"

"I stayed up half the night, you see, finishing a book on just this subject."

"Past lives?"

"Yes! Right here. Well, part of it is in Wales and part in England. London. Near Muswell Hill."

"Let's keep moving," I said. No way was I going to tell her I'd just stayed at Muswell Hill. I'd never get on the train.

"You see, it's about these paintings –"

"Vivian," I said interrupting her just as we got to the great black engines nosed up against the concrete. "Something just occurred to me. You're going to put me on Welsh TV, right?"

"Yes. If they don't cut this bit, which I don't think they will."

"Could I add a statement about my research? A request for information?" This possibility set my heart pounding.

"I'm not sure," she said. "It's not the usual tourism angle."

147

"I know, but it would be a chance for me to reach lots of people and someone out there might be connected to Jane or someone else in her story."

"I'll have to ask my boss," she said. "If he agrees, I'll leave a message at your B & B. Then I could tape you over the phone."

"Thanks," I told her, sensing from her tone that this would never happen.

"My thanks to you," she said. "And look for that book. It's called –"

But the loudspeaker called "All aboard!" and I ran through the wool-clad crowd to the train.

31

As we sped north toward Crewe – the train had to cross into England on this trip – I considered my request to Vivian. Probably nothing would come of it, but in case her boss said yes, did I really want to go public with this quest? The prospect of actually declaring what I was up to was unnerving. "Research" was a respectable cloak but I knew that I was naked underneath. However, a book would be plenty public, I told myself. You can't hide forever from what you're doing.

But maybe a little longer?

To distract myself from this question, I pulled out of my briefcase a ziploc bag of quotations I'd put together. "Vitamins," I call them, and often make up a batch as a gift for writer friends. Seated on the crowded, swaying train, I drew out a folded strip of paper which when stretched out bore these words from Emily Dickinson:

The world is not conclusion;
A sequel stands beyond.

I shivered in the overheated air. *Dead But Still Speaketh* the stone read. Am I Jane's sequel? I know she has spoken to me. Just not the way I wanted, not the way I hoped.

Maybe in olden days you could ponder such things in the quiet of a train car, but not in the era of cell phones. Across from me a young woman named Sarah who was drinking a mid-morning beer shattered my attention by ranting to Gavin about a recent hangover.

Out the window, sheep with blue-daubed backs were running in fields of the tenderest green. Then the train barrelled through Shrewsbury, a red stone church streaming past. "The world is not conclusion." Could I declare that to my fellow travelers: the handsome woman reading and, with her little finger, picking her teeth? the mother who said to her toddler, "Relax now. If you don't stop it, I shall shout and slap you about the legs"? the college student sleeping with his brown curly head thrown back and a bag of crisps open in his lap? Could I say, 'You will live again. I'm doing it. I've come from Kentucky to trace a long-ago life'? I did not know. I still don't.

The snack trolley bumped and rattled nearby. "Cheese and onion," the steward replied to an unheard inquiry. Behind me, a man said, "I remember. I remember!" and I strained to hear what memory had accosted him, but from another seat a loud-voiced young woman with dark hair in braids like Dorothy Gale suddenly blurted to a companion, "He's just saying, like, 'You're going to be mine whether you like it or not.'"

Amid this welter of voices, I gave up trying to think. Instead I bought a sandwich from the trolley. "Sutherland," the label said. "Suitable for vegetarians. Mature cheddar and red leicester with mayonnaise and spring onion on malted brown bread." It was as good as its words, and I kept the label as a souvenir.

Not until I got home and was sorting through the Royal Post bag I'd stuffed with such scraps from my trip did the synchronicity of that label hit me. *Sutherland* was supposed to be Ruth's married name, the identity I could find no trace of. And it had shown up on the train, dropping a hint in my lap and a sandwich in my belly.

Following a stopover at Crewe, I read and dozed the rest of the way until the train suddenly swung out of mountains and along the flat silver expanse of Colwyn Bay. Looking out over the water I felt my spirits rise like the birds riding the gray sky. Soon I would stand on that bridge!

From the train station at Betws-y-Coed it was an easy walk to Coed-y-Fron, the B-and-B from which I planned to get a cab to Llanrwst. Once settled, I asked Mike the proprietor to make the call for me, but he said he was headed north on an errand and would be glad to drop me off on his way. There was a local train back on the hour. I relaxed. This was so easy! It was handed to me.

Mike's route turned off some distance from the bridge, so I got out and followed a footpath beside the winding river. Though the sky hung gray, occasional gusts of wind shoved the clouds apart and let in some sun. That happened just as I rounded a bend and saw the bridge. Yellow light poured over the gray stone with its three wide arches, the tallest in the middle, creating a center point. From photographs I knew that a medallion marked this spot, and all at once I was sure Jane had stood there, had put her hand on that stone. But why? Why would she have come all this way?

The guidebook said Betws-y-Coed was a haven for painters in the nineteenth century, so maybe that was it. Maybe she came to paint the rich hills of Snowdonia, the famous waterfall. And Llanrwst. Why not?

I reached the edge of the bridge. On my side was the little town; on the other was the cottage which had the crimson roof in the jigsaw puzzle. Now in February it boasted only dead vines. The bridge, too, was an ordinary scene, bustling with cars, lorries, a school mini-bus, and people walking. But when I put my foot on its sidewalk, something happened. A charge prickled the air. Moving forward, I took my first sure steps on that side of the ocean. And I heard Laura's voice steadying me, as it had over invisible bridges that brought me here: "One, you step onto the bridge. You feel the stone under your feet. Two, you begin to move forward. Three, you see that the center of the bridge is shrouded in mist . . . ."

I looked. The center of the bridge was a double line of vehicles. Still I felt myself alone on the trance bridge too. I walked on, the busy going-home traffic of 1999 extraneous, like a shawl I could put off if I wanted to. And when I reached the center, when I stood at the overlook the peak of the bridge afforded, the cage of time vanished. I had been there, I was there. Long ago. Now. Someone was with me, someone – oh, I could feel his energy, his warmth, someone I was coming to love. Together we were looking at the river, pewter water spangling over rocks, and he was turning toward me, about to speak . . . .

Then nothing. A horn honked. A lorry shifted gears behind me. I stood alone.

'My God,' I thought. 'My God. I have come back.'

32

I came off the bridge and walked through the little village of Llanrwst, but it might as well have been a movie set for all the reality it held for me. Though I saw the craft shop and the Red Lion pub, the Welsh wool store and the parish church, all I could think of was that moment on the bridge. I had been waiting for Jane to appear to me somehow, through a place or an artifact; it hadn't occurred to me that I might become her. Maybe she had been waiting for me to make that surrender. Maybe I had to be standing where she stood.

In a daze I bought a few gifts in the craft shop and asked directions to the train. I was almost giddy riding back to Betws-y-Coed, and celebrated with a delicious (and expensive) lamb dinner and trifle at a nearby inn.

But that night when I got into my white enameled bed, I found myself in tears. I'd been up since 5:45, done the TV interview, made the long journey, found the bridge.

That's where the tears came from: from that meeting, from her presence and her absence and the man with her, whom she loved and who I could feel died ahead of her. My

154

chest was heavy with her sorrow. I felt bereft of a whole gone world.

But I took myself in hand. It was time for me to be thinking about getting back to my own life. Tomorrow the train ride back to Swansea – during which I had to draft a speech I was to give for the National Council of Teachers of English two days after I got home – and then packing and settling up to leave for London the next day. I wanted to stop and see Robert and Betty, and to give myself a buffer between all that had happened in Wales and my return to Kentucky.

As I suspected, there was no message from Vivian waiting at Heatherlands. That's just as well, I thought. How in the world would I turn this search into a soundbite for the telly? Besides, it could elicit replies from hecklers and crackpots.

In my room I sorted through piles of stuff, setting aside a stack of books and papers for mailing home en route to the train. That would lighten my load considerably. Then I unpacked my briefcase and repacked my suitcase, did a little yoga, and fell into a jumbled sleep.

The next morning Bertie drove me into town, very talkative all of a sudden, reminiscing about his service in the RAF, boasting about swimming every day from Pobbles to Three Cliffs and back. He took a different route from the bus, and as we swung around one curve I saw a cottage that called out to me. Before I could ask him about it, there was another curve with a church set in it. He told me the name of the church but couldn't identify the cottage. I'd follow up on this. A few minutes later, Bertie and I said goodbye at the post office. How lucky, I thought, how lucky I was to stay with these kind people.

155

As the train pulled out of Swansea – *Abertawe* in Welsh – I felt sad and blessed, confused and a little exalted. Jane had met me in Cymru, though not in any way I had imagined. And what I would make of it when I got home I had no idea.

33

The trip home went smoothly, but before I got over jet lag I had to leave again to give the speech I'd drafted on the train. Back from that excursion, I came down with a cold that further muddled my transition from travel to home. Steve was eager to know what had happened, what I had found in Wales, but somehow I was unable to tell him. It was too much, too little, too specific, too vague – and most of all, too far away. Every day that passed the miles between me and Cymru, me and Jane, multiplied. Not only did I not come home with a communicable answer, I was empty of questions, too.

Then I received a note from Emma Jones. "I came across this obituary when looking for something else," she wrote. "Isn't that how it goes?"

With interest but little expectation, I read the memorial words for Ruth/Jane's mother, Lucy Campbell Teeple:

Corning Journal, October 25, 1882
Died in Campbell, Monday, October 8th, Mrs. Lucy
Teeple, aged 92 years. She was born in Stillwater,
Saratoga County, New York, May 5, 1791.

So began a rich account of her life. Nothing about her missing daughter, of course, though it did mention her faithful servant Jane or "Aunt Jen." Then I came to the last paragraph:

> . . . *The volume of such a life is not closed at death. Its pages will be examined and read with tearful eyes and the sacred lessons they inculcate will exert a moulding influence over the lives of surviving friends. "She, being dead, yet speaketh."*

I felt like I was falling backward off a ledge. I'd never seen this epitaph anywhere until it grabbed me in the Aberfan Garden of Remembrance. How could the same words be here?

Had I recognized it in Wales because the Jane part of me had read it in her mother's obituary? Was it used in Bath because it was used in Wales – an inherited epitaph? I took a deep breath. I had been wrestling with this story long enough to know that I couldn't answer that question. To know that it's beyond me. It's all beyond me. Maybe, I thought, sitting at my dining room table, the rest of the mail avalanched around me, maybe it's time to quit trying to figure this out. Time to take the story Jane has given me and see what else she has to say.

Upstairs in my writing room, I cleared my desk, setting aside what I'd written about my search, and pulling out all the pieces I'd written in Jane's voice. Some were almost direct transcriptions from the past-life sessions, others elaborated on events she had mentioned there, and still others were completely new material. I'd already placed them in a rough

158

chronology. Now as I read through, I flagged the spots where there were pieces missing. I would concentrate on writing these words, I decided. I would try hear her story whole.

It felt good to have a plan and clear work to tackle instead of all this thrashing about I'd been doing. And, honestly, it was a relief to turn from the confusion of my search to her voice. It let me take a step back.

You can imagine my surprise when, before telling her story, Jane stepped into mine.

Words
for
Jane Grace

1

Circles of light led me to her. Like stepping stones on the grass alongside the cliff-top path to Rhossili. "Let's follow those," I said to my companion, and we did, my hand in the crook of his arm, him going on about the sea grass, the saxifrage . . . . I love his words, but this day their portent fell away as we walked, and their sound became like the waves pounding, like the surf, the sea.

Once in the circle, what I saw before me was not the salt-washed grassland high on Gower, open on all sides to the work of water below, but the little landlocked park called Pulteney Square, an ocean and a life away in Bath, New York. I stood by the fountain. A little girl was running toward it, toward me, wearing nothing but the scarcest undergarments – little short drawers and a chemise, not white or ivory-hued, but bright yellow and blue. Who had let her out in that condition? She was small, perhaps four or five, and though I had been gone from that town for fifteen years, I felt I must learn who she was and take her home.

Not wanting to frighten her, I sat on the fountain's

edge. My friend says I stopped stone-still in the field and sat down. He spoke to me and I made no answer. The little girl was close now. There was something familiar about her, dark eyes bright, brown hair bouncing loose from whatever held it back.

She slowed down as she reached the stone rim, the circle of the fountain, and without a word scrambled into my lap. I put my hand on her head, which was hot and damp from running, looked at the scuffed knees, her small feet in blue cloth tie-on shoes. Before I could speak, she put her hand in the dancing water and, through the shock of it, she shimmered into me, flowed into my bones the way your soul dizzies up when you look long at the night sky. That little one took her place in me and there was nothing to hold back or question.

But there were other people at the fountain now – a boy, a man, a woman. They too were familiar in some way and very strangely clad. Short pants for the boy, who was much too old for them, and not enough covering for the woman's arms and legs. Seated beside me on the edge of the fountain, they must have been the little girl's family. Just as I recognized this, the mother said, "How do you know about this place?"

And from my mouth, in a small, high voice, in the park where I had once chased butterflies, where strands of my life are woven like the ribbons in the Maypole dance, came the words: "I used to teach school here."

2

I still see him. Here I sit, a world away, a stack of my students' copy books on the table before me, and I see Marshall's hands: large but fine-boned, his nails flat not rounded like mine, his wedding ring gleaming. I see the knob of his wrist where the shirt cuff has slid up. I see his cufflink, silver, engraved with MWR like waves. He is reaching across the table for my hand and I am stunned. It is like the story of storms which I tell the children: warm collides with cold. Jolted, I do not pull back. I lift my gaze from his hand to his face.

Marshall's eyes are so blue, and his thin face is caught between joy and anguish. Down the hall, Caroline, his wife, is in bed as she has been off and on for six years, with bouts of intense pain and paralysis. I have brought soup and flatbread for their supper. My mother used to do this task, taking her turn on the list of church women who pray and cook for shut-ins. But Mother broke her hip at New Year's and cannot yet leave the house, though she made the soup, redolent of cabbage and tomatoes.

This is my third turn at carrying in the food. Each time Marshall has accepted it graciously, asked about my students, my hope of spring flowers (he loves a garden too), and my mother's health. This day, because of rain falling in sheets, now straight down, now sideways, and because his tea kettle whistled as he came to the door, he invited me to join him for tea.

Knowing Marshall from the school office and admiring his compassion, his care of Caroline, his never indicating by word or gesture, the shell his life has become, I did not hesitate.

"Thank you," I said. "I am a bit chilled."

So we sat, sharing the amber tea, breathing in bergemot, eating scones with "a modicum of jam," as he put it. We were speaking of our town -- how it has changed since his childhood, ten years before mine, how he once tried to sled off his father's shed roof and separated his collarbone -- when suddenly he sighed and said, "We are alike, you know," and reached for my hand.

His touch cast over my whole being an invisible net of stars. Not just my body felt this heat, this illumination. In an instant, my wandering became a path, a journey to one moment. I put down my cup, reached across the scones on their cobalt plate, across my life islanded, and took his other hand, the one with the ring.

3

And then, after a little rapture, I was with child. A spinster. Forty-three.

Soon after I knew, I agreed to marry Leander Sutherland, a widower who had been courting my mother for me for years. Leander was a decent man – a doctor of sorts. (I say *of sorts* because I never saw him demonstrate much acuity, witness the fact that he did not perceive any change in me.) If I was drawn to him at all, it was as one would be to a good sofa – well-built, well-upholstered – that was Leander. But do not expect a sofa to give light.

So when he traveled from Galesburg to Bath for his semi-annual proposal dinner, I passed him my life with the roast I could not eat, saw in the mashed potatoes our rumpled bedclothes, and with that certainty felt part of me go dizzy and rise, spinning, into the chandelier.

That is the part of me that dreamed another life, that fashioned escape out of other peoples' memories – Maggie, the hired girl's story of coming over from Ireland, alone and poor, unskilled; Gwen Jones' mother's misty recollections of

Wales. Marshall was willing to help me plan what to do, but I had been too shocked to do it until I accepted Leander. Then I was all motion. I could not let myself become furniture.

I made one last visit to Marshall's house, carrying potato soup and a loaf of brown bread. I had made the soup myself, telling Mother she needed to rest after the full dinner she had prepared for Leander the night before. Truth be told, I wanted to have for once the privilege of feeding Marshall and, as I stood in Mother's narrow kitchen, cutting potatoes and onions on the scarred board, I let myself pretend – only for a moment – that I was his wife, that later, when evening slanted its light through the long window, he would walk through the door and I would taste his mouth before I tasted soup, that we would talk – how easily our days flowed together! – and that the baby coming would be our common joy.

I thought what a gift if Caroline should die (as the doctor had told Marshall she might) and leave us free to have that extraordinary life, so common that most people never contemplate having any other. I was too lost in my longing to be shocked by this thought.

But once the soup was simmering, I scraped this fantasy with the peelings into the pail and forced myself to imagine another scene: standing in my own kitchen on the far side of the sea, preparing this same soup for the child and me, serving it with a story of the father she never knew, the father, I decided, who had been killed in a fall from a horse, and whose house I had left because I could not bear the memories.

This resolve I took with the soup and bread to Marshall's. We sat in the parlor, a room which before I had only passed through. I knew his table, with its amber vase of dried field flowers, and I knew his bed. But the parlor with its claret-colored rug and watergreen furnishings was unfamiliar. It was good to meet on new ground.

I told Marshall I would marry Leander for my mother's sake, and then, as soon as possible, make by escape. I did not say that he could join me when Caroline died, but felt it understood. I would let him know my whereabouts and the baby's arrival. That would be enough.

"If you're certain that is what you want, I will book your passage," Marshall said. "But if you stayed, you would come home to your mother in the summers. I could see you – and the child."

I shivered. "You know I cannot do that."

He nodded.

"You would not want me if I could," I went on.

Anguish thickened his voice. "Ruth, I would want –"

"Stop!" I said, my hands in front of me, fingers splayed, palms out. "We cannot do this!"

Silence. The pulse of the grandfather clock. A few chirps from the finch he kept in Caroline's room.

"You will need another name," Marshall said, his voice smooth now, his thin face composed. "Just so there are no questions."

I had considered this already. "I will take Jane Grace," I told him.

"But is that not . . .?"

"Our servant's name, yes. But she was a slave; there was no birth certificate. And it will be a link to this life, an anchor."

"Which I cannot give you," he said.

"But you will," I insisted. "Acquiring the ticket, you will give me the name."

He pressed his lips together as if to bridle pain. He lifted a paperweight, a glass iris, from the low table between us. "I will need some kind of document," he said, not looking at me.

"I can provide that," I told him. "We have paper for certificates at school. I can forge something."

"Forge?"

"I am an excellent copyist," I boasted, then smiled at my tone.

"I did not know that," he said, and my heart was seized with pain at all he did not, could not know.

"I could draw this," I said, taking the paperweight from his hand. It held his heat.

"Ruth," he began, reaching as if to touch my shoulder.

"It's Jane," I said, standing. "I will bring the document to your office, along with the date for the wedding. We will have a . . . an excursion afterward. I could leave a month after our return."

"Yes," he said, standing as well. "Let me see you to the door."

Together we moved through the still room to the hall where he lifted my cloak from a coat stand and held it out. Like grief, it settled on my shoulders.

I turned to face him. "The soup will need heating," I said. "Remember." I opened the door myself, afraid to risk the reach of his arm around me. Stepping out, I saw a world grown dark, the moon cradled in the trees.

4

It was a silvery, rain-struck day when I departed – summer rain. I left early, having sent a trunk on ahead to the boat. The note for Mother I'd mailed to my brother's address.

The night before, my husband had watched me pack a valise of clothes to make over into costumes for the church play. At the train station the porter saw me set off alone for a brief excursion. They saw what they expected. But I was leaving for good. And I was not alone. Inside me grew a life even newer than the one I hoped to claim.

I had begun to feel her move. The sensation was uncanny: quick as a minnow, a grace note. At first I thought, 'This can't be it. So fast and light, almost imagined.' But there it was again, like a flash of wing.

I could not have gone without her. She was my ticket, my companion.

How can I say how my heart was that day – high as a hallelujah, low as a grave?

My clothes, of course, did not fit. Like my name, they

were familiar but no longer useful. Ruth I had to put away, like my rose dress with white tucks in the yoke. "It won't meet," we say of a skirt, a blouse. My name wouldn't meet either. Wouldn't meet people on the ship or strangers who might become friends across the ocean. Ruth Sutherland might be taking an excursion to see her brother. Jane Grace was emigrating to Wales.

So the baby would bear the name Grace too. If a boy, I thought to call him Marshall, after his father. That would be safe so far away. Lucy, if a girl: my mother's name.

My memory of the voyage is lit by the overhead lamp swaying, pitching in the opposite direction from the ship. The swing of light and shadow added to my queasiness, but I was never sick. A mercy. As I held on tight in my berth in the night, I told the baby, "You have got the ocean for your cradle, little one. The deep blue sea."

And it did look blue by moments. But it could show a hundred other colors as well: emerald, olive, silver, gun gray, black. I have seen water coral pink at sunrise shine orange and purple at day's end. Old gold, turquoise, lightning white – all are tricks light plays on water. The voyage taught me this.

And I thought how strange it is, how false, that when we teach children colors, we name red, blue, green. We do not say these are categories of color, each the lid to a marvelous paintbox. We might as well teach them only *bird* and count it sufficient for *warbler, phoenix, finch*. My child shall know better, I vowed. My students shall not be so blind. With my students I have been able to keep that vow.

I did not scorn the Captain's solicitousness nor mind

the other passengers' murmuring, "A shameful state. Isn't it pitiful? Sent off like that." I knew I was not pitiful, but blessed.

And when Lucy and I docked in Bristol, on a day of high winds and bright skies, I was pleased to come down the gangplank heavier, with a slower gait than I had gone up. Everything was as it should be. We had crossed over. All that was lacking was a home.

5

Part of that home I found in Anna Siery, who happened upon me the day I arrived. Through the years of our friendship, she loved to tell the story:

"A mystery it is to me always, how you came alone with the baby about to be born. It didn't take the Sight to know you needed a friend.

"You should have seen yourself: small as you are, in that gray cloak, looking like you were carrying the earth ball beneath it. Dark red hair piled up in an inexplicable American fashion, face too small for your body, and a perfect horror of a hat."

"I adored that hat!" I said laughing.

"There was nothing to do but love you," she replied. "I just chanced to pass by – it was a Sunday and I had been to Mass – as the cab drew up at the Sea Mist Hotel. First I saw a doorman wrestling with your trunk and then you wavering as you stepped down to the curb. I didn't realize your condition at first. Thought you must be faint or dizzy and so I stepped in to offer my arm. Close up, I saw your pallor and plight of your body and well, my heart went out to you. Poor creature. What a dreadful state!"

"Surely I was not quite so pathetic!" I protested.

"No, now, I never said pathetic. It's quite proud you were. Though I walked with you into the lobby, you declined my offer to help you settle in."

"I did agree to meet for tea the next afternoon," I reminded her.

"Praise the saints is what I say! That first day I was too hesitant to mention the source of my concern. Now I would just straight-out say, 'Come, lamb, and tell me what brought you to this fix, and what you plan to do after the blessed event.'

"Of course, you could have had a husband arriving on the next train, but somehow I knew you did not."

Monday afternoon, when we met over tea and a plate of scones, Anna looked me in the eye and said, "You'll be needing a doctor."

"Not for a while yet," I replied. "And a midwife will do."

"I expect it would be good to have a doctor check your general health a bit sooner," she insisted.

"Might you recommend someone?" I asked, spooning clotted cream onto a scone. Now that I was on dry land, I was ravenous.

"Dr. Jones," you answered. "Gareth Jones. I think you will like him."

"I like you," I said, much to my surprise. "You are a Godsend, Anna Siery. How lucky for me that you were walking by!"

"It's the way I always go," Anna said. "And it is my pleasure to know you. You are –" Suddenly she hesitated, stirring her well-stirred tea. "You are the first American I have ever known."

"And you," I said, my heart lightening, "are the first friend of my new life."

6

I had been in Swansea almost a month when my trouble started. I was at the market, just above St. Mary's, buying some fruit to take back to the room I had rented from Mrs. Powrys three days earlier. I was looking at apples when I felt it: a dull ache in the small of my back, as if I was about to get my courses. It's from standing too long, I thought, with this great weight in front. I shall buy three apples, go back to my room, and lie down. I was always buying three of things. I thought it was for blessing (the Trinity, good things come in threes) but hours later, when the pain was really upon me, I looked at those apples and knew that I was buying threes to feed my family: Marshall, the baby, and me.

Any other time this would have brought tears, but in labor I could not afford them. Instead I let this be kneaded into the body's pain, another wave dragged in, pulled under, only to rise and gather, break over me again.

I was not alone. When I returned from the market, I asked Mrs. Powrys if someone could be sent for Anna, who lived in the Uplands, some distance from High Street. By the time I knew I was bleeding, she was there.

We had only just met, of course, but our acquaintance was clearly becoming friendship and I had meant to tell her, before the baby came, that my condition was one of hope, not of shame. But we were past such conversation when she arrived at the rooming house.

Anna was not a nurse; her training, like mine, was as a teacher. Nor had she borne any children herself. But her clear heart seemed to tell her what to do. She got me up from where I was lying on my side, had me into my nightgown and back into bed before I could say 'I can't move.' I felt strength and calm flow into me through her hand on my upper arm.

"When should this baby be coming?" she asked, wiping my face with a cool cloth.

"Not for three months," I told her.

"And have you had others?"

"No," I said. I might have told her everything then, but the pain left no room for story. Soon it wiped out even my fear that the baby was too young to live.

There was more blood than my usual bandages would stanch, and I began to be twisted by each grasp of pain, the breath wrung out of me.

"I must go and speak to Mrs. Powrys," Anna said. "You need to be in hospital."

"Do not leave me!" I begged, hands clasping her hands, eyes clasping her face.

One hand let go and fished in her pocket. Then she was pressing beads into my grasp.

"Hold this, and the Blessed Virgin will watch over you," she said. "I will come right back."

But my memory stops with the click of the door behind her. It holds nothing of being carried down the stairs, of the ride to the hospital, the doctors, the actual birth.

Like a gate, memory clicks open again on Anna's face above me, her brown eyes shiny.

"God be praised," she said. "We have not lost you too."

7

They did let me see her, Lucy, my beautiful red-haired baby, eyes and lungs shut like a bud. She never breathed. Never opened. No one keeps their children, I know that.

But when the day dawned foggy in a Swansea hospital, and a Matron showed me the Beginning and the End all at once, I thought it was God's judgment: as I left my mother and Marshall, so my daughter would leave me. Not some forty years later but on the first day.

The doctor wrote in a clear, ornamented hand:

Lucy Grace   Stillborn

She had been so full of motion! How could she be still?

Was it on the roll of the ocean, in some blissful swim, that the cord wrapped around her neck? Did it lie there like a necklace until birth slid it into a noose?

It is customary, when a child dies at birth, to see the event as a great disappointment: something long prepared

179

for did not happen. Someone almost was.

But Lucy *was* – there is no almost. She danced. She dreamed. Feet on my ribs, she stretched her legs, causing me pain and laughter. Her steadiness soothed me. Her exuberance lightened me. Her promise gave my dark days hope.

I know her eyes were blue. They all begin that way. But were they navy blue like my father's or like Marshall's, blue as a vein inside the wrist?

For a long time, I felt that if only she had looked at me I would not feel so alone.

Why, Little One, why did you turn back at the gate? Lucy, your name means light. Open your eyes!

It took a while to realize those words were for me. "I gave you all I had," Lucy told me. "I carried you over. You're free now. It's you should open your eyes."

And gradually I did. It was trying to find the blue of her eyes that started me painting. Oh, I put it in the water, painting seascapes, but it was her gaze I searched for. Once, alone on the coast, I shouted into the waves, "I'm your mother. Look at me!" But what I heard was, "I'm your mother. Look for yourself."

And slowly, by rock flower and child's face, I did. There came to me again that crashing joy I remembered from childhood, that all-lost-and-found feeling you get lying eye-level with the grass. As a child, it is your birthright. As an adult, it is forgiveness. That flood of wholeness melts the heart the way mineral spirits take darkened varnish from paint. Lifts the film so vermillion, azure, celadon shine through. So she gave me life, my Lucy did, though I was supposed to give her hers. Gave me passage.

I sent Marshall a card which said *No roses* and signed it only *JG*. I knew he would know from the code we had worked out: yellow rose, the baby is a boy; a girl if I wrote pink rose.

Marshall had no children – his wife had always been ailing – and the promise of this child was dear to him. He was a good man. I could not fault his love or loyalty. I know he grieved, took tea to his wife, and went on. I only wish I could have shared with him what she gave me, could have told him how she lived on.

I longed to send him a painting but could not do that. And of course I had no news of him. Did not know until after Mother's death that he had died too: Marshall. And his wife survived him. Died childless, they would say, but not so. He had a daughter no one in New York ever knew of. We had a daughter: Lucy, light of the sea.

8

Once I had recovered from the birth and secured a job at Kittle School, Anna helped me find a place to live nearby. It was old when I came to it, my house. Many souls had been born and died where the thatch showed between the roof beams. Yet I, accustomed to a genteel dwelling of inlaid floors and beveled glass back in America, felt my heart settle as soon as I stepped through the low doorway onto the slate floor.

Just inside that door, on the thick wall of the lintel, were two carved figures, a man and a woman. Not kneeling, they nevertheless seemed to be in prayer. "Guardians against evil spirits," Anna told me. "No doubt there is a rowan tree in the garden as well." And so there was, its berries being another protection.

The whitewashed walls, inside and out, seemed to me ancient and perfect for a house scoured by the sea. But Anna said most likely it was red when it was new, for evil will not come into a red house.

I could not imagine evil dwelling here, whatever the color, in a place so spare and simple and free. Or was it my own freedom I was feeling, I who had cared first for father, then for mother, who until I went on shipboard had never lived a day on my own?

I had not wanted to be alone. I had wanted Lucy to wed me to home and hearth. But that dream is lost, I told myself, as I stood in my cold and musty parlor. I must make a house for me, then, for the woman I have traveled this far to become. For Jane I will get on my knees and build a fire now. For Jane Grace I will make a nest.

9

Eleven pupils I had the first year. We struggled together – they with little English, I with less Welsh. I focused first on the broadest things, naming the elements of our landscape, the change of season around us. I learned the Welsh words, too, though it was against the rule. Soft and guttural, they sounded like German a sure hand had sanded down.

Language had never been my gift. When I was a schoolgirl, Latin slid from my mind like those little ones skittered down a slick slope. But this learning was different. Words were the road between the children and me – my side English, theirs Welsh – and everything depended on our being able to travel.

Friend (*ffrind*) we taught each other; path (*llwybr*), bird (*aderyn*), book (*llyfr*), sea (*mor*). Each day, new words, new horizons: read (*dorllen*), help (*cymorth*), sing (*canu*).

I can say it now: I was a better teacher for having lost Lucy, my *merch*, my *baban*. She attached me to this earth with a strength I'd never experienced. Everything multiplied in intensity and possibility. The sky could never be just blue;

bread had a hundred tastes. And now I saw that the children I taught were all distinct souls, loved fiercely by someone and loaned to me. Unlike Lucy, they were buds who *bloomed.* But they came from the same miracle, the force that grows to water and light straight through the rock.

10

It was at St. Mary's, Pennard, that I met Albert. A visitor was an event in our small parish, especially one who came alone, and there he was, in his dark brown trousers and rusty tweed coat, red-gold hair curly but close-cropped and beard flourishing. Solid as a mountain, blue eyes alive with delight. He had about him a force – a man would have felt it too – *for life*. His outline was hopeful, unwearied. Since I sat near the back of the church, I saw him come in and then watched him throughout the service: the ease with which he smiled and nodded to those around him, the energy with which he knelt and rose.

Though it was August, the church kept a chill. I had been shivery before Albert joined us. Not so, after. Did my bones remember ahead the heat he would teach them?

He did not go to Communion, an omission no doubt noted by all twenty gathered faithful. I expected him to vanish when Mass ended, and lingered in my pew to see. But no, he spoke easily to Father Hopkin at the door, then stood at his side for introductions.

"Jane Grace, our schoolmistress," Father Hopkin said as I approached, hand shielding my eyes for the passage from dark into light.

Albert reached to shake my hand, then clasped it in both of his. This gesture took my breath. Unexpected, too forward, delicious.

"I'm Albert Croft, Miss Grace," he said. "A surveyor."

"A pleasure to meet you," I replied. "Will you be with us long?"

Smiling broadly, he said, "That depends on a number of things."

I let myself look straight at him. His beard was curly, too, and with his clear eyes and ruddy skin, made a bright face altogether.

Depend on me, my heart beat, pulsing through my hand to his. *Depend on me.*

11

It was May when Albert asked me to go with him up to Llanrwst. He wanted to see the old bridge. Being a surveyor, he was passionate about how land and man-made structure go together. He wanted to stand at various points and do sitings of the juncture, feel the weight of building stone against dirt. But perhaps I should say that being a surveyor, he was interested. Being Albert, he was passionate.

So, having kissed him only twice, both meetings of smiles, not of hunger, I said yes. We took the train up to Colwyn Bay on the Irish Sea, then hired a cab for the short trip south. Our rail journey had veered into England, which bruised my heart. When I had passed through England before, Lucy had been alive.

Albert noticed the shift in my mood. We were sitting side by side, with me next to the window. He chuckled, nudged my upper arm with his shoulder. "Ah, Janie," he said, "you are a Welshwoman already. The sight of England clouds your face!"

"The land is lovely," I said. "It's your lawmakers I have

trouble with."

Albert himself is English, a Geordie, born up near Scotland, between the Teays and the Tyne. And being the person he is, such facts are significant. Those rivers made him: their music, their power, the necessity that they be bridged.

I never picture Marshall out-of-doors. I saw him there, of course, walking in the village, but he appeared, as most people did, to be passing from enclosure to enclosure. His gardens were small, close to the foundation, ornamenting the house.

So I was not prepared for Albert. Although all his labor was for building, it was the land that held him. Buildings he shrugged off like cumbersome overcoats when he got outside. Of inclement weather he took no more notice than of dust in the parlor. What was sleet compared to rock high on the Gower cliffs, the wild ponies running, the waves headlong below?

Back in New York we had a poet whose spirit reminds me of Albert. *Leaves of Grass* he wrote. In my old life, I found his long lines, like arms always outstretched, distasteful, common. But in Albert's great heart I saw that it is not at all common: a man at home in this world, delight with tree and waterfall rushing through his body like blood.

We talked of English arrogance, setting out to rob the Welsh of their own tongue.

"My students make their way around it," I told him. "They do what they call Talking Underhand."

"Meaning?"

"In free time, they hold a hand between nose and mouth, parallel to the ground, and speak Welsh beneath it. If I ask them something, they lower the hand to the neck, as if cutting off the head, and speak English."

Albert rested his hand at an angle across his chin. I wondered how that plush beard felt. With thumb and forefinger he parted his moustache as if giving his mouth more room for words. Finally he spoke.

"I would venture it's the body they are cutting off with English," he told me. "Their own words are rooted in their flesh."

I pointed out that you can't cut off one without cutting off the other.

"Too many words," Albert said.

It was dusk by the time we arrived. There was no lodging in Llanrwst, so we stayed that night at The Royal Oak in Betws-y-Coed, a larger town four miles south. Without consultation, Albert booked two rooms. I was disappointed and relieved. I had watched him differently on the trip up, thinking I might get to know that strong, sweet body.

In the hotel dining room, we had a lovely meal of lamb, new potatoes and peas, with crème brulee for dessert. "They feed the angels this," Albert said. "It strengthens their wings."

Next morning we breakfasted and walked the five miles to Llanrwst. From the footpath along the river we could see blackberries and mayapples in bloom, and all the green world was tender. I loved the walking. This freedom was not given to women where I came from – this leave to enjoy the motion and power of your body, to travel. I told Albert this.

"And what do the ladies do Away Over?" I liked his crooked phrase for my homeland. It seemed to suit my past as well.

"We sew," I said. "We cook, teach, tend the sick, put up food, plant flowers. Basically we are indoor creatures. What we can't scrub we polish."

"The Lord's pity," he said.

The Conwy being a twisty river, we were near the bridge by the time we saw it: three generous arches of gray stone, the middle one being the largest, the walls meeting in a peak at its center. I was praising the grace of the arches when Albert said, "But look how it rises gradually from the banks, as if it grew there. The bridge appears not sudden or imposed, but natural, arising from the landscape itself. And this was built in 1636."

I knew then why we had two rooms. He wanted nothing sudden or imposed in our joining either. The late May morning was billowy. My heart felt like the sun in my chest. We stood in the center of the bridge, facing the river, lorries and buggies and walkers passing behind us. Albert paused in his discourse on the breakthrough this bridge represented, the turn from medieval heaviness, and I turned too, rose on my toes, and kissed him. Not a peck, like a thrush gives something shiny in the grass, but a drinking kiss like a mouth over a fountain.

When I drew back, Albert looked bemused, then beamed. He grabbed me in his strong arms and kissed me till I was not quenching a thirst but drowning.

"Albert!" I cried, pulling back to catch my breath.

He nuzzled my neck. "Architecture!" he said.

12

Albert was so unlike Marshall. Florid where Marshall was pale, alive to the edge of his skin, while Marshall governed his body like a kingdom. Albert's kingdom was out there: rivers and hillocks, slopes, grades, the properties of rock. If Marshall's eye was on the abstract horizon, Albert's was on all that lies between.

So Marshall surveyed the minds of men he must work with while Albert surveyed the land, reckoned what it would take to bridle it with a railroad, a canal.

It follows, then, the difference in their hands. Marshall's thin, tapering fingers moved delicately up my back, over my breasts as if he were playing a sonata. Albert's fingers were thicker, the right palm callused from reins and walking stick, and he took my body up the way a hungry man takes bread. Direct, not rough. Already knowing the substance he wanted.

Albert could laugh at us tangled and driven. It was his pleasure to laugh. Marshall only whispered. And would have, I am sure, even had there been no Caroline. For Marshall's passion was all proportionate, like a letter folded to fit its envelope, sealed with a judicious tongue. Albert's was a wild sky and a peppering of sea, wind rapturous at the long grasses, parting them to reveal the spurred bloom.

Albert's old jacket, heather-gray tweed – my hands open, palm arched back as I think of it. The thorny scent of his pipe smoke, his russet hair silver streaked, except for his moustache, which kept its black flecks, and made his mouth more a cave of words or a furnace to be stoked with food, made it shaggy with mystery, blackberry dark, and muscular as thunder.

13

And so I settled into the richest time of my life, with Albert as lover, Anna as sister, my students as challenge and joy. And I had painting, too: the gift grief had given me. Years passed fast as clouds in a west wind. I was certain I would someday tell Anna my story, and she would forgive me and counsel me about how to tell Albert. I did not see this as mere possibility but as a sure moment, a way-station on the road ahead.

Through the years, I shared family news, supposedly borne by letters: "My mother's heart grows weaker, but her spirit is steady." "David, my brother, will soon retire." "Oh my, what a winter they are having in New York!" I would say. "Mother writes that snow has covered the cast iron fence."

How I longed for that to be true: for a blanket of transformation, however cold, however temporary, to soften the barrier between us!

I had written David soon after I arrived in Wales, giving my new name and address and begging his forgiveness. I had asked him to tender this to Mother and advise whether I might write to her.

His reply was swift, inscribed in black ink on a black-bordered card. There was no salutation, but then perhaps he could not decide between *Ruth* and *Jane*. *Sister*, I thought. He could have written *Sister*. Instead, six words:

We look upon you as dead.

I cried myself sick, then read it again, recognized the card, and laughed a broken laugh. David, the boy who stole dinner rolls and hid them in his pillowcase, who kept his lead soldiers in a tin with a lid so tight my small hands could never get it off, David had hoarded his share of the mourning cards I bought after Father's death. He was doling them out one dire circumstance at a time!

David's note arrived in the winter of 1874, before grass had covered the scar of Lucy's grave. After that I invented loving letters. I thought I was doing it for Albert and Anna, so that they might not guess the truth. I see now that I myself was consoled by the lie.

Thus I was stunned, eight years later, to receive a real letter from home. Not from David nor Mother, but from Sarah, my sister-in-law. It was addressed to Jane Grace and appeared to be written in haste. Inside, pretense had been abandoned. *My Dear Ruth,* it began, and my hot tears with it.

David has forbidden me to write, yet I must let you know that your mother died peacefully on the 8th of October. Burial as expected. Our sons are grown. I have missed you all these years.

Sarah

195

14

All that spring – our last one – Albert wanted to go to Cornwall. I told him to go on, I was done with England. But Albert persisted. "Cornwall is not really England," he said. "It has palm trees, love. When you are there, Buckingham Palace seems as remote as America."

It was for the railway Albert wanted to go. The line had finally been extended from St. Erth to St. Ives. Years ago he had surveyed a possible route but the government had ruled the cost of building too burdensome. Now that it was done he wanted to see if the train followed his old plan.

I refused all spring and the better part of summer. So much to do for my students, I said. It was too cool for a journey. Too hot. I didn't want to leave my garden.

"You are not getting old, are you, Janie?" he asked me in August.

"Albert Croft, you know you are years nearer Heaven than I am!"

"Then why have you grown wary of traveling on earth?"

"I went to St. David's with you at midsummer," I pointed out.

"Gone and back in a day's time. You could have done it in a push-chair."

"Albert!" He was saying this to vex me, I knew, yet I could not help myself from being vexed. Did he not recall the real reason I dreaded English soil? Must I drag my heart out for him to see again? Sometimes I think you might as well love a rock as a man! But then I do relish light and sea spray on stone.

"It is Lucy," I told him. "It is that heart-sickness I do not want to return to."

"'Tis been ten years!" he exclaimed.

I was speechless. He had a child, a grown and living son, and still he could not comprehend my loss.

He looked at me, concern clouding his blue eyes. "Would your little one want her death to rob you of Cornwall? The light in the ocean there – blues and greens not in your paint box. Would she not want her mama to see that?"

Tears took me, and then Albert's arms. The next day he bought our tickets.

CR

He was right, of course. It is a different sea at St. Ives. The light – there is so much of it! And the intensity of turquoise and teal fairly dazzles the eyes. As soon as we were settled in the hotel, I thanked Albert for persuading me to come. This wasn't England. Not only palm trees but bougainvillea burgeoned like dreams among the steep-stacked whitewashed houses. We arrived in early evening to find painters with their easels set up on the beach and the fishermen bringing in their battered boats, nets full of tumbling silver.

Come morning I declined the shore path walk he was setting out for. "The day is so clear," I told him. "I want to rest and sketch." At first I feared he would declare he should stay with me – he could crowd a soul that way sometimes – but his better judgment or the call of sea cliffs kept him to his course.

Thus I was alone when I strolled along the beach not far from the little railway station. Kissed by sea mist and stunned suddenly by how easily I could still be walking in Pulteney Square back in Bath or shut up in Leander's house in Galesburg with a husband less luminous to me that the sand beneath my feet. It was a miracle, truly, that had carried me from that life to this. And the miracle, I saw at once, was not only Lucy but Marshall. Marshall Reid, whose deep satiny voice and slender hands I had almost forgotten.

Heat flashed over my limbs just as it had when those hands first discovered me, when Marshall, in a a passion that was part moral anguish, woke me into this world. His lips were the most delicious thing I had ever tasted. And when I said his black hair, already gray speckled, was beautiful, he said it was like a chalkboard a child had not washed well. Not so, I told him. It was like a tiger lily. Foolish, but I wanted to say that to me he was not of the school but of the garden. It was, after all, the love of gardens that brought us together. That and our hungry hearts.

I had not gone far before I came upon a group of bathers. Children from near-grown to one barely walking, and a bearded man tall and straight and thin as a young tree. The baby, naked, was toddling in the surf when he picked her up, held her eye to eye a moment and then threw her into the sea. Such shrieks as she flew through the air and then as he scooped her out of the froth. Were they delight or terror? Horrified, I looked at him again. He looked as old as I was. Had he once tossed those strapping lads into the perilous water too? Were they laughing out of remembrance?

"Good morning!" I called out as I went by.

Assorted voices answered. They were scrambled in the surf.

The father handed the baby to the oldest girl, who walked toward me, then set her sister back near the edge of the tide. She did this with a gentleness as intense as the father's exuberance. "There you go, Ginny," she said.

I felt as though I had come upon a scene from a play. There was something so arresting about them. As I walked on I realized what it was: we are all like that baby thrown by God into tumult, dependent on someone to pluck us up until we have the strength to save ourselves from drowning.

CR

And then that autumn Albert died. Such a light, such a light went out, I cannot tell you. Hiking alone, he fell and was not found till morning. Besides a broken ankle he had cracked ribs and bruised lungs. Pneumonia set in. After nine days he was gone.

Anna was with me. But Anna herself was failing. Not her body, grown stout and stooped, but her mind. Once when we were keeping vigil through the night, she thought it was her father tossing and moaning there beneath the sheets. Junius Seary, dead in Ireland fifty years before.

Albert had moments of clarity to the last. And he always knew me. When I touched his hand, he grew calmer, and when I spoke he squeezed my fingers. So light then, the grasp of that strong hand. Letting go.

All along I had meant to tell him my story, to give him my true name. But there was no time. And Anna – Anna was past comprehending. Some days I had to remind her I was Jane. Learning Ruth would have been beyond her. When I buried Albert there was no one to tell but the priest.

15

This will stay with me always. I am in a small stone church, my parish church. It is Friday afternoon and I have come, as always, for Confession.

I feel very strange, still caught in last night's dream. I was out walking in a wet field. My throat hurt. And – I cannot explain this – I wanted to fly. There was some sound I longed to make, something I wanted to join. My throat still hurts and my head spins from looking up into the whirling sky.

I enter the confessional and kneel, ready to say the words, familiar as coins I drop in the candle box. But what I say, what pushes up from my heart and twists my voice is, "I am not Jane Grace."

The story comes in a rush and I try to tell the priest all of it. But I begin to weep and, though I slow my words and moderate my voice, I can feel him pulling back, feel distance open between us like a pit. Then the door creaks and someone leans in and puts an arm around my shoulders, drawing me out. Soothing, she calls the name, "Jane, Jane." And I tell her I am not Jane. Her eyes are full of pity.

We go outside and sit on a bench in the churchyard. I know this woman. Her husband is the green grocer. She is always here on Fridays, her string bag shriveled on her arm.

"You are not yourself today," she says. "Just not yourself." Laughter breaks through my tears and her face goes pale. Do I need her to "see me home?" she asks. Home?

At last I have told the truth and there is no one to believe me. I could have told Albert. I might have told Anna. But I feared their rebuke, their turning away. Now they are gone. And this disguise, this shift I meant all along to discard, is my soul's last garment. I will take it off only for God.

16

Hoofprints, each a deep C, in the sparse grass at the cliff's edge. Christ's Church Calling. Hoofbeats, heartbeats. Wild horses could not drag me to the church door. I tried to tell them who I was. I tried to confess the long lie of my life only to be laughed at. Only to be led out, labeled addled.

God is not the Church. I doubt this day He could even get in, so stuffed it is with flowers and candles, so swamped with singing. Resurrection. I remember my grandfather's church in Campbell. C C C. See him now, preaching, who would be hounded out over some squabble among the faithful. Church is a wheel of cheese. Sometimes you get a full slice, other times a sliver, a peel of rind, or a whiff of the knife. I cannot go there to be fed. Cannot commit Communion, though all these years I have knelt and opened my mouth, a cup to receive the Host.

Now I must make my communion alone, here on the cliff edge. Alone as I Crossed the ocean and lost my Child, alone as I Chose my life.

17

An old woman, I had gone back to Aberdulais where Albert and I had once spent a weekend. He had wanted me to see that spot, where two rivers and two canals meet. Not canals he had surveyed – these were laid out before his time. But he admired the curve of the Tennant towpath bridge and the the aqueduct across the River Neath.

Eleven years after his passing, I took a notion to see those canals again. I went by train to Neath and then set out on foot, following the river to the village. I was a walker. Not feeble, but no longer spry.

As I came in sight of the towpath bridge I was thinking of how bridges marked our life together, from our first real kiss at Llanrwst to bitter words on the Castle Bridge at Cardiff, to the sweetness of our moments here, where I had proclaimed this stone curve "the loveliest!" and Albert had whispered, "Tis nothing to your breast!" I had gone all red and delighted. He could say a thing like that, his lips wet with words almost like a kiss. I cannot explain it.

So I stood again on that towpath bridge and made my

communion, scattering the bouquet of larkspur I had bought at the station. But when I opened my eyes and looked down at the purple spikes landing in green water, I saw something else, something even then I knew I could not see. Tilted, resting on the river bed, was a golden plate. It was broken – I could see that too – maybe a third of it gone. And it pulled my heart – I know no other way to say it – it pulled my heart to the sky so that my shadowy body in its brown traveling dress was tilted like the plate and then laid back on the grass. I do not remember falling.

Then I rose up out of myself, my heart calling me as a bird calls to its mate. I was at once in the air and on it, as mist or cloud must be. And I sped over fields and rivers and little towns, back to Swansea, stained with the fires of metal-making, on down the rough glory of the Gower, till I beheld my own house, cradled in its curve at Pennard.

I saw the white-washed walls, my kitchen garden, the thatched roof, plush and soft as a nest. And oh, it was so beautiful! Beloved. But the air I was in, the air I *was*, swirled and thickened around *Goodbye*. It was almost said of me. Till something at the center, something that was not yet air, cried *No!* and my heart rushed back.

Heavy now, and broken as that gold plate, it pushed me backward, faster and faster, the land below a blur of green and stone and rivers, till I was crushed into my body, back on the moorland outside Aberdulais, where I lay with a great pain over half my chest. Lay while the sky swirled aqua, then rose, then black. I tried but could not rise, for half of me, the half that would not let go, had turned to stone.

And I spent the last of my days like that, only my right

side moving, barely able to speak. Stroke, they called it.

18

After the stroke, I was taken to hospital and then to a rest home, paid for, I presume, by my teachers' pension. Having slammed death's door because I could not bear to leave my house, I never again spent a night under its roof. I do not know what became of it.

Through several seasons I lingered. Snow came to the window, then blossoms. I would not take Communion, so the priest ceased calling. For a while I was visited by a few known souls, but they faded. Perhaps they grew tired. Perhaps they passed on ahead.

Then came a morning when I opened my eyes and felt awake, awake as I had not been in many years. I could not speak clearly and my writing hand was useless, so when the attendant came, I gestured with my left, scribbling wildly on the air until finally she propped me up, and fetched paper, pen, and a board to bear on.

I intended to write "I am not Jane Grace," but the *not*, the knot, would not come. Instead, in spider-silk letters, wobbly as a new colt, I wrote only "I am." Like a sweet wind, those words billowed through me, and I felt my spirit released, freed. Dizzy, I spun upwards. I scooted along the blue ceiling, knowing I would find a door or curtain or gate. And when I did, it was tendril green, tender as morning. I breathed in, it breathed open, and I passed through.

Answering

Eleven years have passed since I first returned to Bath. During that time I've followed a ghost down all the roads you've read about, and some others besides. My brother's and my parents' memories led me back to that little town, and then someone else's tears washed through me on a Sunday morning at St. Mary's. Trying to unravel that experience led me to past-life voices, faded census books, airline tickets, Welsh cliffs. My journey was chasing something I could almost see, losing it, and giving up only to have it come up from behind and touch my elbow. It was all the details of my story that matched records I could find and all the ones which didn't. It was writing and rewriting, finding a structure, throwing it out, starting over. It was looking everywhere for a book like this, which would give me a model for what I was trying to do, only to realize there wasn't any. The book I wanted to read was the one I had to write.

So where does this journey of words, miles, and memories leave me? The truth is it doesn't leave me. It's not over and it may not be over even when I die.

It's possible, though unlikely, that some reader will be a descendent of Leander Sutherland and send me furious proof that Ruth Teeple married him and never set foot on any ship larger than a rowboat. I don't see how this could be, since I found no evidence of their having lived in Galesburg, but who knows? Eyes are wobbly; records, incomplete. I could have missed a crucial piece of information.

Then what?

Then I would have to think Jane told this story for a purpose. Maybe it's the life she longed to have; maybe she offers it to me as a sign of the great wide world out there, as a call to come and see how big my life can be.

She got me across the ocean, after all. She got me to make a trip alone I would never have dreamed of making otherwise.

And what if, as one friend suggested, Jane is not a separate person at all but an aspect of my present self calling me to grow, to change old habits in midlife?

If that were true, it would raise further questions about all the coincidences I've chronicled here. And it would still leave me in the presence of Mystery and interconnectedness which I believe to be the heart of all our lives. If Jane is an aspect of my current self, as opposed to a past one, she is still a soul voice calling me to greater possibility. And while the distinction – between past-life voice and present inner one – would have been crucial to me when I started out, at this point I don't much care. She is what she is, and I'm not going to be able to *solve* her, anymore than I can solve other people in my life. Like the whole experience, Jane is complex and defies categories. She is and we are connected, and that connection is richer than I will ever be able to spell out.

While I may have missed something in the Galesburg Library, or in other archives, that refutes the story I tell here, it's also true that I know I've missed things in my own avalanching archives here that confirm it. For example, after

I finished the previous draft of this book in 2005, I was looking through a journal I kept during the past-life sessions and I found this entry:

> *10/6/97   Maybe Jane Grace calls me because I'm not finished with that life, that guilt, and carry the paralyzed part with me (and may pass it on to my children). The guilt, the fear of leaving.*
>
> *We went up to her death but not necessarily through —she seemed caught, held up somehow, maybe in a coma or a Bardo state.*
>
> *I won't narrate the whole story since I need to type it up [from the tape] but the most powerful moments were when she was dying and looked down on her house, when she saw … her father, and when I saw the stone church lit from within with a glow which I knew was her heart.*

This was followed by a drawing of the church:

Something about that drawing looked familiar but I didn't know why. I began hunting through files. Had I been to this place? Had I seen a picture of it?

When I left Swansea on St. David's Day, 1999, Bertie, the B & B proprietor, drove me to the train. He took a road different from the bus route, a road I'd never been on before. We passed a cottage set back from a curve and I could feel it pull at my heart. Then before I could get words out about that, we careened by a church.

"What's that?" I asked Bertie.

"St. Mary's," he said.

"Do you know anything about the cottage before it?"

"Which one?"

It turned out there were several, though I hadn't noticed. I did have the church name, though. The same as the Catholic Church in Bath where I'd cried Jane's tears. But there are St. Mary's churches everywhere. That hardly counts as coincidence.

What did count, though, was the architectural drawing on the church pamphlet they later sent when I wrote to them:

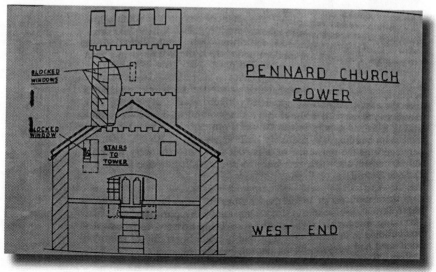

It matches the drawing I had made two years earlier. It matches what I saw in a trance.

Not until I was proofreading this manuscript did I notice that all the churches named St. Mary's – in Bath, Swansea, and Pennard – matched the name of the hospital where my father died, my father whose death prompted this journey.

☙

What does all this mean: the synchronicities? the wild correspondences? the equally impressive points at which the pattern falls apart? Is it an elaborate example of how the creative mind works, noticing every connection and making the most of it, inventing fictions for what does not fit? You could say that. If I had seen a different name on the boat ticket in the past-life session, would I have found that name in the census? Possibly. And would she have been an unmarried schoolteacher? Certainly they were numerous. She could have left Bath, too, and perhaps I would have been off following her. It doesn't seem likely, but I can't say.

All I can do is offer you my experience, the journey of an enthralled yet skeptical pilgrim who learned, among other things, how limited our powers of explanation are, how reductive our labels. I use the words *past-life experience* because they're handy, but it's sort of like saying 'Give me that thingamajig,' when you want a one-and-three-eighth's inch diamond core drill bit. The trouble is that I don't have the right words. To some extent, words are answers. If I called for that drill bit, I would know exactly what I was doing. As it is, I began this search with a mysterious experience and ques-

214

tions and ended up with a lot more of both.

Past-life therapy is what you call the technique where I found and spoke a lot of Jane's story, so it wears that cloak. But the life is not the garment, as Jane herself says. Life is mystery. We are mysteries to each other: parents, lovers, children, friends. The tree in our dooryard, the book in our hands.

Something calls us, daily, to our deepest selves. Jane, whoever and however she is, called me, and I am thankful that I had the chance to answer. Thank you, dear reader, for taking this journey with me. I hope it speaks to you about the depth of your own.

OPENING

There are tricks in Time, slicks and slogs,
patches where Time exaggerates itself;
there are sinks, balds, caves, and paths
crossing as on any mountain.
This is how I found myself at age five,
remembering for a woman of forty-three,
how waves of 1870 drifted into a '52 Ford.

The *juzzz* of tires on pavement,
car rocked like a cradle by curves,
turns into the trance of travel
and for a moment overrides Time.

And I remember the fountain at the center,
source of life ever-flowing,
water which is as it was for the woman
who so long ago was once five too.
I put my hand in.
Laughter splashes in two times.
Blood rushes through two hearts.
Time ravels out on the mountain,
and an old soul steps into Now.

Poet, novelist, and children's author George Ella Lyon works as a free-lance writer and teacher in Lexington, Kentucky. Her most recent books include *No Dessert Forever!, Trucks Roll!, Sonny's House of Spies,* and reprints of *Catalpa* (poems) and her adult novel, *With a Hammer for My Heart.*

For more information, go to www.GeorgeEllaLyon.com.

Printed in the United States
94880LV00007B/385-405/A